INSIGHT PUBLICA®

INSIGHT PUBLICA®

Kozhikode, Kerala, India
www.insightpublica.com
e-mail: insightpublica@gmail.com
Title: The Golden Book of the Dutch Navigators
Author: Hendrik van Loon
(English)
First Insight Publica Edition: May 2022
Book Design: kjvj@insight

ISBN 978-93-5517-246-4
Printed and Published by Insight Publica
for InsightinPublica Printers & Publishers Pvt. Ltd.

THE GOLDEN BOOK OF THE DUTCH NAVIGATORS

Hendrik van Loon

INSIGHT PUBLICA

Hendrik Willem van Loon (January 14, 1882 – March 11, 1944) was a Dutch-American historian and journalist.

Born in Rotterdam, he went to the United States in 1903 to study at Cornell University. He was a correspondent during the Russian Revolution of 1905 and in Belgium in 1914 at the start of World War I. He later became a professor of history at Cornell University (1915-17) and in 1919 became an American citizen.

From the 1910s until his death, Van Loon wrote many books. Most widely known among these is The Story of Mankind, a history of the world especially for children, which won the first Newbery Medal in 1922. The book was later updated by Van Loon and has continued to be updated, first by his son and later by other historians.

However, he also wrote many other very popular books aimed at young adults. As a writer he was known for emphasizing crucial historical events and giving a complete picture of individual characters, as well as the role of the arts in history. He also had an informal style which, particularly in The Story of Mankind, included personal anecdotes.

Contents

FOR HANSJE AND WILLEM

This is a story of magnificent failures. The men who equipped the expeditions of which I shall tell you the story died in the poorhouse. The men who took part in these voyages sacrificed their lives as cheerfully as they lighted a new pipe or opened a fresh bottle. Some of them were drowned, and some of them died of thirst. A few were frozen to death, and many were killed by the heat of the scorching sun. The bad supplies furnished by lying contractors buried many of them beneath the green cocoanut-trees of distant lands. Others were speared by cannibals and provided a feast for the hungry tribes of the Pacific Islands.

But what of it? It was all in the day's work. These excellent fellows took whatever came, be it good or bad, or indifferent, with perfect grace, and kept on smiling. They kept their powder dry, did whatever their hands found to do, and left the rest to the care of that mysterious Providence who probably knew more about the ultimate good of things than they did.

I want you to know about these men because they were your ancestors. If you have inherited any of their good qualities, make the best of them; they will prove to be worth while. If you have got your share of their bad ones, fight these as hard as you can; for they will lead you a merry chase before you get through.

Whatever you do, remember one lesson: "Keep on smiling."

HISTORICAL INTRODUCTION

The history of America is the story of the conquest of the West. The history of Holland is the story of the conquest of the sea. The western frontier influenced American life, shaped American thought, and gave America the habits of self-reliance and independence of action which differentiate the people of the great republic from those of other countries.

The wide ocean, the wind-swept highroad of commerce, turned a small mud-bank along the North Sea into a mighty commonwealth and created a civilization of such individual character that it has managed to maintain its personal traits against the aggressions of both time and man.

When we discuss the events of American history we place our scene upon a stage which has an immense background of wide prairie and high mountain. In this vast and dim territory there is always room for another man of force and energy, and society is a rudimentary bond between free and sovereign human beings, unrestricted by any previous tradition or ordinance. Hence we study the accounts of a peculiar race which has grown up under conditions of complete independence and which relies upon its own endeavors to accomplish those things which it has set out to do.

The virtues of the system are as evident as its faults. We know that this development is almost unique in the annals of the human race. We know that it will disappear as soon as the West shall have been entirely conquered. We also know that the habits of mind which have been created during the age of the pioneer will survive the rapidly changing physical conditions by many centuries. For this reason those of us who write American history long after the disappearance of the typical West must still pay due reverence to the influence of the old primitive days when man was his own master and trusted no one but God and his own strong arm.

The history of the Dutch people during the last five centuries shows a very close analogy. The American who did not like his fate at home went "west." The Hollander who decided that he would be happier outside of the town limits of his native city went "to sea," as the expression was. He always had a chance to ship as a cabin-boy, just as his American successor could pull up stakes at a moment's notice to try his luck in the next county. Neither of the two knew exactly what they might find at the end of their voyage of adventure. Good luck, bad luck, middling luck, it made no difference. It meant a change, and most frequently it meant a change for the better. Best of all, even if one had no desire to migrate, but, on the other hand, was quite contented to stay at home and be buried in the family vault of his ancestral estate, he knew at all times that he was free to leave just as soon as the spirit moved him.

Remember this when you read Dutch history. It is an item of grave importance. It was always in the mind of the mighty potentate who happened to be the ruler and tax-gatherer of the country. He might not be willing to acknowledge it, he might even deny it in vehement documents of state, but in the end he was obliged to regulate his conduct toward his subjects with due respect for and reference to their wonderful chance of escape. The Middle Ages had a saying that "city air makes free." In the Low Countries we find a wonderful combination of city air and the salt breezes of the ocean. It created a veritable atmosphere of liberty, and not only the liberty of political activity, but freedom of thought and independence in all the thousand and one different little things which go to make up the complicated machinery of human civilization. Wherever a man went in the country there was the high sky of the coastal region, and there were the canals which would carry his small vessel to the main roads of trade and ultimate prosperity. The sea reached up to

The Cocos Islands

his very front door. It supported him in his struggle for a living, and it was his best ally in his fight for independence. Half of his family and friends lived on and by and of the sea. The nautical terms of the forecastle became the language of his land. His house reminded the foreign visitor of a ship's cabin.

And finally his state became a large naval commonwealth, with a number of ship-owners as a board of directors and a foreign policy dictated by the need of the oversea commerce. We do not care to go into the details of this interesting question. It is our purpose to draw attention to this one great and important fact upon which the entire economic, social, intellectual, and artistic structure of Dutch society was based. For this purpose we have reprinted in a short and concise form the work of our earliest pioneers of the ocean. They broke through the narrow bonds of their restricted medieval world. In plain American terms, "They were the first to cross the Alleghanies."

They ushered in the great period of conquest of West and East and South and North. They built their empire wherever the water of the ocean would carry them. They laid the foundations for a greatness which centuries of subsequent neglect have not been able to destroy, and which the present generation may triumphantly win back if it is worthy to continue its existence as an independent nation.

CHAPTER I
JAN HUYGEN VAN LINSCHOTEN

It was the year of our Lord 1579, and the eleventh of the glorious revolution of Holland against Spain. Brielle had been taken by a handful of hungry sea-beggars. Haarlem and Naarden had been murdered out by a horde of infuriated Spanish regulars. Alkmaar—little Alkmaar, hidden behind lakes, canals, open fields with low willows and marshes—had been besieged, had turned the welcome waters of the Zuyder Zee upon the enemy, and had driven the enemy away. Alva, the man of iron who was to destroy this people of butter between his steel gloves, had left the stage of his unsavory operations in disgrace. The butter had dribbled away between his fingers. Another Spanish governor had appeared. Another failure. Then a third one. Him the climate and the brilliant days of his youth had killed.

But in the heart of Holland, William, of the House of Nassau, heir to the rich princes of Orange, destined to be known as the Silent, the Cunning One—this same William, broken in health, broken in money, but high of courage, marshaled his forces and, with the despair of a last chance, made ready to clear his adopted country of the hated foreign domination.

Everywhere in the little terrestrial triangle of this newest of republics there was the activity of men who had just escaped destruction by the narrowest of margins. They had faith in their own destiny. Any one who can go through an open rebellion against the mightiest of monarchs and come out successfully deserves the commendation of the Almighty. The Hollanders had succeeded. Their harbors, the lungs of the country, were free once more, and could breathe the fresh air of the open sea and of commercial prosperity.

On the land the Spaniard still held his own, but on the water the Hollander was master of the situation. The ocean, which had made his country what it was, which had built the marshes upon which he lived, which provided the highway across which he brought home his riches, was open to his enterprise.

He must go out in search of further adventure. Thus far he had been the common carrier of Europe. His ships had brought the grain from the rich Baltic provinces to the hungry waste of Spain. His fishermen had supplied the fasting table of Catholic humanity with the delicacy of pickled herring. From Venice and later on from Lisbon he had carried the products of the Orient to the farthest corners of the Scandinavian peninsula. It was time for him to expand.

The rôle of middleman is a good rôle for modest and humble folk who make a decent living by taking a few pennies here and collecting a few pennies there, but the chosen people of God must follow their destiny upon the broad highway of international commerce wherever they can. Therefore the Hollander must go to India.

It was easily said. But how was one to get there?

Jan Huygen van Linschoten was born in the year 1563 in the town of Haarlem. As a small boy he was taken to Enkhuizen. At the present time Enkhuizen is hardly more than a country village. Three hundred years ago it was a big town with high walls, deep moats, strong towers, and a local board of aldermen who knew how to make the people keep the laws and fear God. It had several churches where the doctrines of the great master Johannes Calvinus were taught with precision and without omitting a single piece of brimstone or extinguishing a single flame of an ever-gaping hell. It had orphan asylums and hospitals. It had a fine jail, and a school with a horny-handed tyrant who taught the A B C's and the prin-

ciples of immediate obedience with due reference to that delightful text about the spoiled child and the twigs of a birch-tree.

Outside of the city, when once you had passed the gallows with its rattling chains and aggressive ravens, there were miles and miles of green pasture. But upon one side there was the blue water of the quiet Zuyder Zee. Here small vessels could approach the welcome harbor, lined on both sides with gabled storehouses. It is true that when the tide was very low the harbor looked like a big muddy trough. But these flat-bottomed contraptions rested upon the mud with ease and comfort, and the next tide would again lift them up, ready for farther peregrinations. Over the entire scene there hung the air of prosperity. A restless energy was in the air. On all sides there was evidence of the gospel of enterprise. It was this enterprise that collected the money to build the ships. It was this enterprise, combined with nautical cunning, that pushed these vessels to the ends of the European continent in quest of freight and trade. It was this enterprise that turned the accumulating riches into fine mansions and good pictures, and gave a first-class education to all boys and girls. It walked proudly along the broad streets where the best families lived. It stalked cheerfully through the narrow alleys when the sailor came back to his wife and children. It followed the merchant into his counting-room, and it played with the little boys who frequented the quays and grew up in a blissful atmosphere of tallow, tar, gin, spices, dried fish, and fantastic tales of foreign adventure.

And it played the very mischief with our young hero. For when Jan Huygen was sixteen years old, and had learned his three R's—reading, 'riting, and 'rithmetic—he shipped as a cabin-boy to Spain, and said farewell to his native country, to return after many years as the missing link in the chain of commercial explorations—the one and only man who knew the road to India.

Here the industrious reader interrupts me. How could this boy go to Spain when his country was at war with its master, King Philip? Indeed, this statement needs an explanation.

Spain in the sixteenth century was a magnificent example of the failure of imperial expansion minus a knowledge of elementary economics. Here we had a country which owned the better part of the world. It was rich beyond words and it derived its opulence from every quarter of the globe. For centuries a steady stream of bullion flowed into Spanish coffers. Alas! it flowed out of them just as rapidly; for Spain, with all its foreign glory, was miserably poor at home. Her people had never been taught to work. The soil did not provide food enough for the population of the large peninsula. Every biscuit, so to speak, every loaf of bread, had to be imported from abroad. Unfortunately, the grain business was in the hands of these same Dutch Calvinists whose nasal theology greatly offended his Majesty King Philip. Therefore during the first years of the rebellion the harbors of the Spanish kingdom had been closed against these unregenerate singers of Psalms. Whereupon Spain went hungry, and was threatened with starvation.

Economic necessity conquered religious prejudice. The ports of King Philip's domain once more were opened to the grain-ships of the Hollanders and remained open until the end of the war. The Dutch trader never bothered about the outward form of things provided he got his profits. He knew how to take a hint. Therefore, when he came to a Spanish port, he hoisted the Danish flag or sailed under the colors of Hamburg and Bremen. There still was the difficulty of the language, but the Spaniard was made to understand that this guttural combination of sounds represented diverse Scandinavian tongues. The tactful custom-officers of his Most Catholic Majesty let it go at that, and cheerfully welcomed these heretics without whom they could not have fed their own people.

When Jan Huygen left his own country he had no definite plans beyond a career of adventure; for then, as he wrote many years later, "When you come home, you have something to tell your children when you get old." In 1579 he left Enkhuizen, and in the winter of the next year he arrived in Spain. First of all he did some clerical work in the town of Seville, where he learned the Spanish language. Next he went to Lisbon, where he became familiar with Portuguese. He seems to have been a likable boy who did cheerfully whatever he found to do, but watched with a careful eye the chance to meet with his next adventure. After three years of a roving existence, with rare good luck, he met Vincente da Fonseca, a Dominican who had just been appointed Archbishop of Goa in the Indies. Jan Huygen obtained a position as general literary factotum to the new dignitary and also acted as purser for the captain of the ship.

At the age of twenty he was an integral member of a bona-fide expedition to the mysterious Indies. Through his account of this trip, printed in 1595, the Dutch traders at last learned to know the route to the Indies. The expedition left Lisbon on Good Friday of the year 1583 with forty ships. During the first few weeks nothing happened. Nothing ever happened during the first weeks on any of those expeditions. The trouble invariably began after the first rough weather. In this instance everything went well until the end of April, when the coast of Guinea had been reached. Then the fleet entered a region of squalls and severe rainstorms. The rain collected on the decks and ran down the hatchways. A dozen times or so a day the fleet had to come to a stop while all hands bailed out the water which filled the holds. When it did not rain the sun beat down mercilessly, and soon the atmosphere of the soaked wood became unpleasant. To make things worse the drinking water was no longer fresh, and smelled so badly that one could not drink it without closing the unfortunate nose that came near the cup.

On the whole the printed work of Jan Huygen does not show him as an admirer of the Portuguese or their system of navigation. In all his writing he gives us the impression of a very sober-minded young Hollander with a lot of common sense. Portugal had then been a colonial power for many years and showed unmistakable signs of deterioration. The people had been too prosperous. They were no longer willing to defend their own interests against other and younger nations. They still exercised their Indian monopoly because it had been theirs for so long a time that no one remembered anything to the contrary. But the end of things had come. Upon every page of Jan Huygen's book we find the same evidence of bad organization, little jealousies, spite, disobedience, cowardice, and lack of concerted action.

When only a few weeks from home this fleet of forty ships encountered a single small French vessel. Part of the Portuguese crew of the fleet was sick. The others made ready to flee at once. After a few hours it was seen that the Frenchman had no evil intentions, and continued his way without a closer inspection of his enemies. Then peace returned to the fleet of Fonseca.

A few days later the ship reached the equator. The customary initiation of the new sailors, followed by the usual festivities and a first-class drunken row, took place. The captain was run down and trampled upon by his men, tables and chairs were upset, and the crew fought one another with knives. This quarrel might have ended in a general murder but for the interference of the archbishop, who threw himself among the crazy sailors, and with a threat of excommunication drove them back to work. Half a dozen were locked up, others were whipped, and the ships continued their voyage in this happy-go-lucky fashion. Then it appeared that nobody knew exactly where they were. Observations finally showed that the fleet was still fifty miles west of the Cape of Good Hope. As a matter of fact, they had passed the cape several days before, but did not discover their error until a week later. Then they sailed northward until they reached Mozambique, where they spent two weeks in order to give the crew a rest and to repair the damages of the equatorial fight. On the twentieth of August they continued their voyage until the serpents which they saw in the water showed them that they were approaching the coast of India. From that time on luck was with the expedition. The ships reached the coast near the town of destination. After a remarkably short passage of only five months and thirteen days the fleet landed safely in Goa.

Jan Huygen was very proud of the record of his ship. Only thirty people had died on the voyage. It is true that all the people on board had been under a doctor's care, and every one of the sailors and passengers had been bled a few times; but thirty men buried during so long a voyage was a mere trifle. In the sixteenth century, if fifty per cent. of the men returned from an Indian voyage, the trip was considered successful.

The next five years Jan Huygen spent in Goa with his ecclesiastical master. He was intrusted with a great deal of confidential work, and became thoroughly familiar with all the affairs of the colony. In Goa he heard wonderful tales about the great Chinese Empire, many weeks to the north. He began to collect maps for an expedition to that distant land, but lack of funds made him put it off, and he never went far beyond the confines of the small Portuguese settlement.

Unfortunately, at the end of five years the archbishop died, and Jan Huygen was without a job. As he had had news that his father had died, he now decided to go back to Enkhuizen to see what he could do for his mother. Accordingly, in January of the year 1589, he sailed for home on board the good ship *Santa Maria*. It was the same old story of bad management: The ships of the return fleet were all loaded too heavily. The handling of the cargo was left entirely to ship-brokers, and these worthies had developed a noble system of graft. Merchandise was loaded according to a regular tariff of bribes. If you were willing to pay enough, your goods went neatly into the hold. If you did not give a certain percentage to the brokers, your bags and bales were stowed away somewhere on a corner of a wharf exposed to the rain and the sea. Very likely, too, the first storm would wash your valuable possessions overboard.

When the *Santa Maria* left, her decks were stacked high with disorderly masses of colonial products. The sailors on duty had to make a path through this accumulated stuff, and the captain lacked the authority to put his own ship in order. A few days out a cabin-boy fell overboard. The sea was quiet, and it would have been possible to save the child, but when the crew ran for a boat, it was found to be filled with heavy boxes. By the time the boat was at last lowered the boy had drowned.

The *Santa Maria* sailed direct for the Cape. There it fell in with another vessel called the San Thome, and it now became a matter of pride which ship could round the cape first. Severe western winds made the *Santa Maria* wait several days. The San Thome, however, ventured forth to brave the gale. When finally the storm had abated and the *Santa Maria* had reached the Atlantic Ocean, the bodies and pieces of wreckage which floated upon the water told what had happened to the other vessel. This, however, was only the beginning of trouble. On the fifth of March the *Santa Maria* was almost lost. Her rudder broke, and it could not be repaired. A storm, accompanied by a tropical display of thunder and lightning, broke loose. For more than forty-eight hours the ship was at the mercy of the waves. The crew spent the time on deck absorbed in prayer. When little electric flames began to appear upon the masts and yards (the so-called St. Elmo's fire, a spooky phenomenon to all sailors of all times), they felt sure that the end of the world had come. The captain commanded all his men to pray the "Salvo corpo Sancto," and this was done with great demonstrations of fervor. The celestial fireworks, however, did not abate. On the contrary the crew witnessed the appearance of a five-pointed crown, which showed itself upon the mainmast, and was hailed with cries of the "crown of the Holy Virgin." After this final electric display the storm went on its way.

In his sober fashion Jan Huygen had looked on. He did not take much stock in this sudden piety, and called it "a lot of useless noise." Then he watched the men repairing the rudder. It was discovered that there was no anvil on board the ship, and a gun was used as an anvil. A pair of bellows was improvised out of some old skins. With this contrivance some sort of

steering-gear was finally rigged up, and the voyage was continued. After that, except for occasional and very sudden squalls, when all the sails had to be lowered to save them from being blown to pieces, the *Santa Maria* was past her greatest danger, though the heavy seas caused by a prolonged storm proved to be another obstacle. No further progress was possible until the ship had been lightened. For this purpose the large boat and all its valuable contents were simply thrown overboard.

The recital of Jan Huygen's trip is a long epic of bungling. The captain did not know his job; the officers were incompetent; the men were unruly and ready to mutiny at the slightest provocation; and everybody blamed everybody else for everything that went wrong. The captain, in the last instance, accused the good Lord, Who "would not allow His own faithful people to pass the Cape of Good Hope with their strong and mighty ships," while making the voyage an easy one for "the blasphemous English heretics with their little insignificant schooners." In this statement there was more wisdom than the captain suspected. The English sailors knew their business and could afford to take risks. The Portuguese sailors of that day hastened from one coastline and from one island to the next, as they had done a century before. As long as they were on the high seas they were unhappy. They returned to life when they were in port. Every time the *Santa Maria* passed a few days in some harbor we get a recital of the joys of that particular bit of paradise.

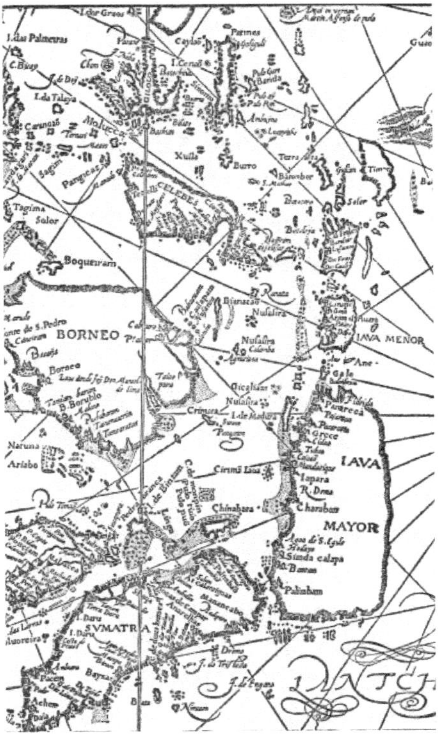

If we are to believe Portuguese tradition, St. Helena, where the ship passed a week of the month of May of the year 1589, was placed in its exact geographical position by the Almighty to serve His faithful children as a welcome resting-point upon their perilous voyage to the far Indies. The island was full of goats, wild pigs, chickens, partridges, and thousands of pigeons, all of which creatures allowed themselves to be killed with the utmost ease, and furnished food for generations of sailors who visited those shores.

Indeed, this island was so healthy a spot that it was used as a general infirmary. After a few days on shore even the weakest of sufferers was sufficiently strong to catch specimens of the wild fauna of the island. Often, therefore, the sick sailors were left behind. With a little salt and some oil and a few spices they could support themselves easily until the next ship came along and picked them up. We know what ailed most of these stricken sailors. They suffered from scurvy, due to a bad diet; but it took several centuries before the cause of scurvy was discovered. When Jan Huygen went to the Indies the crew of every ship was invariably attacked by this most painful disease. Therefore the islands were of great importance.

Nowadays St. Helena is no longer a paradise. Three centuries ago it was the one blessed point of relief for the Indian traders. The diary of Jan Huygen tells of attempts made to colonize the island. The King of Portugal, however, had forbidden any settlement upon this solitary rock. For a while it had harbored a number of runaway slaves. Whenever a ship came near they had fled to the mountains. Finally, however, they had been caught and taken back to Portugal and sold. For a long time the island had been inhabited by a pious hermit. He had built a small chapel, and there the visiting sailors were allowed to worship. In his spare time, however, the holy man had hunted goats, and he had entered into an export business of goat-skins. Every year between five and six hundred skins were sold. Then this ingenious scheme was discovered, and the saintly hunter was sent home.

On the twenty-first of May the *Santa Maria* continued her northward course. Again bad food and bad water caused illness among the men. A score of them died. Often they hid themselves somewhere in the hold, and had been dead for several days before they made their presence noticeable. It was miserable business; and now, with a ship of sick and disabled men, the *Santa Maria* was doomed to fall in with three small British vessels. At once there was a panic among the Portuguese sailors. The British hoisted their pennant, and opened with a salvo of guns. The Portuguese fled below decks, and the English, in sport, shot the sails to pieces. The crew of the *Santa Maria* tried to load their heavy cannon, but there was such a mass of howling and swearing humanity around the guns that it took hours before anything could be done. The ships were then very near one another, and the British sailors could be heard jeering at the cowardice of their prey. But just when Jan Huygen thought the end had come the British squadron veered around and disappeared. The *Santa Maria* then reached Terceira in the Azores without further molestation.

Like all other truthful chroniclers of his day, Jan Huygen speculates about the mysterious island of St. Brandon. This blessed isle was supposed to be situated somewhere between the Azores and the Canary Islands, but nearer to the Canaries. As late as 1721 expeditions were fitted out to search for the famous spot upon which the Irish abbot of the sixth century had located the promised land of the saints. Together with the recital of another mysterious bit of land consisting of the back of a gigantic fish, this story had been duly chronicled by a succession of Irish monks, and when Jan Huygen visited these regions he was told of these strange islands far out in the ocean where the first travelers had discovered a large and prosperous colony of Christians who spoke an unknown language and whose city could disappear beneath the surface of the ocean if an enemy approached.

Once in the roads of Terceira, however, there was little time for theological investigations. Rumor had it that a large number of British ships were in the immediate neighborhood. Strict orders had come from Lisbon that all Portuguese and Spanish ships must stay in port under protection of the guns of the fortifications. Just a year before that the Armada had started out for the conquest of England and the Low Countries. The Invincible Armada had been destroyed by the Lord, the British, and the Dutch. Now the tables had been turned, and the Dutch and British vessels were attacking the Spanish and Portuguese colonies. The story of inefficient navigation is here supplemented by a recital of bad military management. The roads of Terceira were very dangerous. In ordinary times no ships were allowed to anchor there. A very large number of vessels were now huddled together in too small a space. These vessels were poorly manned, for the Portuguese sailors, whenever they arrived in port, went ashore and left the care of their ship to a few cabin-boys and black slaves. The unexpected happened; during the night of the fourth of August a violent storm swept over the roads. The ships were thrown together with such violence that a large number were sunk. In the town the bells were rung, and the sailors ran to the shore. They could do nothing but look on and see how their valuable ships were driven together and broken to splinters, while pieces of the cargo were washed all over the shore, to be stolen by the inhabitants of the greedy little town. When morning came, the shore was littered with silk, golden coin, china, and bales of spices. Fortunately the wind changed later in the morning, and a good deal of the cargo was salved. But once on shore it was immediately confiscated by officials from the custom-house, who claimed it for the benefit of the royal treasury. Then there followed a first-class row between the officials and the owners of the goods, who cursed their own Government quite as cheerfully as they had done their enemies a few days before.

To make a long story short, after a lawsuit of two years and a half the crown at last returned fifty per cent. of the goods to the merchants. The other half was retained for customs duty. Jan Huygen, who was an honest man, was asked to remain on the island and look after the interests of the owners while they themselves went to Lisbon to plead their cause before the courts. He now had occasion to study Portuguese management in one of the oldest of their colonies. The principles of hard common sense which were to distinguish Dutch and British methods of colonizing were entirely absent. Their place was taken by a complicated system of theological explanations. The disaster that befell these islands was invariably due to divine Providence. The local authorities were always up against an "act of God." While Jan Huygen was in Terceira the colony was at the mercy of the British. The privateers waited for all the ships that returned from South America and the Indies, and intercepted these rich cargoes in sight of the Portuguese fortifications.

When the Englishmen needed fresh meat they stole goats from the little islands situated in the roads. Finally, after almost an entire year, a Spanish-Portuguese fleet of more than thirty large ships was sent out to protect the traders. In a fight with the squadron of Admiral Howard the ship of his vice-admiral, Grenville, was sunk. The vice-admiral himself, mortally wounded, was made a prisoner and brought on board a Spanish man-of-war. There he died. His body was thrown overboard without further ceremonies.

At once, so the story ran, a violent storm had broken loose. This storm lasted a week. It came suddenly, and when the wind fell only thirty ships were left out of a total of one hundred and forty that had been in the harbors of the islands. The damage was so great that the loss of the Armada itself seemed insignificant. Of course it was all the fault of the good Lord. He had deserted His own people and had gone over to the side of the heretics. He had sent this hurricane to punish the unceremonious way in which dead Grenville had been thrown into the ocean. And of course this unbelieving Britisher himself had at once descended into Hades, had called upon all the servants of the black demon to help him, and had urged this revenge. Evidently the thing worked both ways.

This clever argument did not in the least help the unfortunate owners of the shipwrecked merchandise. One fine day they were informed that they could no longer expect royal protection for the future. Jan Huygen was told to come to Lisbon as best he could. He finally found a ship, and after an absence of nine years returned to Lisbon. On his trip to Holland he was almost killed in a collision. Finally, within sight of his native land, he was nearly wrecked on the banks of one of the North Sea islands. On the third of September of the year 1592, however, after an absence of thirteen years, he returned safely to Enkhuizen. His mother, brother, and sisters were there to welcome him.

He did not at once rush into print. It was not necessary. The news of his return spread quickly to the offices of the Amsterdam merchants. They had been very active during the last dozen years and they had conducted an efficient secret organization in Portugal, trying to buy up maps and books of navigation and, perhaps, even a pilot or two. They knew a few things, and guessed at many others. A man who had actually been there, who knew concrete facts where other people suspected, such a man was worth while. Jan Huygen became consulting pilot to Dutch capital.

The Dutch merchants still found themselves in a very difficult position. They had to enter this field of activity when their predecessors had been at work for almost two centuries. These predecessors, judging by outward evidences, were fast losing both ability and energy. But prestige before an old and well-established name is a strong influence in the calculations of men. Those who directed the new Dutch Republic did not lack courage. All the same, they shrank from open and direct competition with the mighty Spanish Empire. Besides, there were other considerations of a more practical nature.

The Middle Ages, both late and early, dearly loved monopoly. Indeed, the entire period between the days of the old Roman Empire and the latter part of the eighteenth century, when the French Revolution destroyed the old system, was a time of monopolies or of quarrels about, and for, monopolies. The Dutch traders wondered whether they could not obtain a little private route to India, something that should be Dutch all along the line, and could be closed at will to all outsiders. What about the Northeastern Passage? There seem to have been vague rumors about a water route along the north of Siberia. That part of the map was but little known. The knowledge of Russia had improved since the days when Moscow was situated upon the exact spot where the ocean between

Iceland and Norway is deepest. The White Sea was fairly well known, and Dutch traders had found their way to the Russian port of Archangel. What lay beyond the White Sea was a matter of conjecture. Whether the Caspian Sea, like the White Sea, was part of the Arctic Sea or part of the Indian Ocean no one knew. But it appeared that farther to the north, several days beyond the North Cape, there was a narrow strait between an island which the Russians called the New Island (Nova Zembla) and the continent of Asia. This might prove to be a shorter and less dangerous route to China and the Indies. Furthermore, by building fortifications on both sides of the narrows between the island and the Siberian coast, the Hollanders would be the sole owners of the most exclusive route to India. They could then leave the long and tedious trip around the Cape of Good Hope, with its perils of storms, scurvy, royal and inquisitorial dungeons, savage negroes, and several other unpleasant incidents, to their esteemed enemies.

The men who were most interested in this northern enterprise were two merchants who lived in Middleburg, the capital of the province of Zeeland. The better known of the two was Balthasar de Moucheron, an exile from Antwerp. When the Spanish Government reconquered this rich town it had banished all those merchants who refused to give up their Lutheran or Calvinistic convictions. Their wealth was confiscated by the state. They themselves were forced to make a new start in foreign lands. The foolishness of this decree never seems to have dawned upon the Spanish authorities. They felt happy that they had ruined and exiled a number of heretics. What they did not understand was that these heretics did not owe their success to their wealth, but to the sheer ability of their minds, and before long these penniless pilgrims had laid the

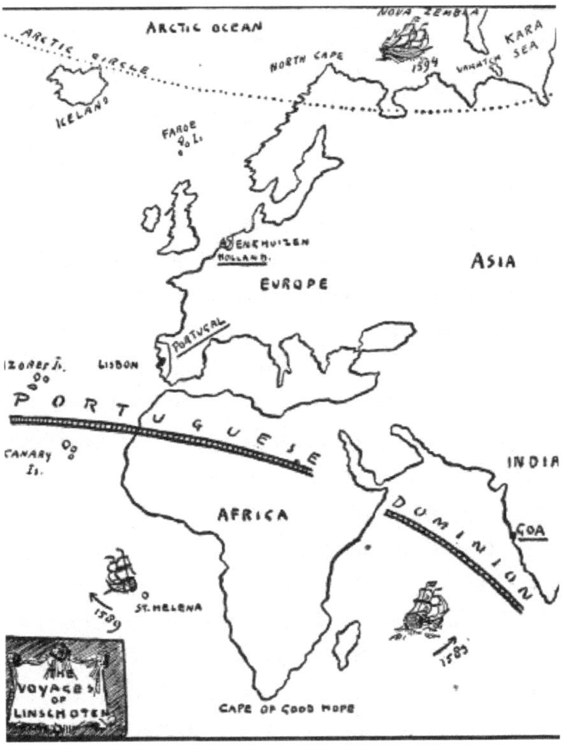

VOYAGES OF LINSCHOTEN

foundations for new fortunes. Then they strove with all their might to be revenged upon the Government which had ruined them.

De Moucheron, one of this large group which had been expelled, had begun life anew in the free Republic and was soon among the greatest promoters of his day. Of tireless energy and of a very bitter ambition, none too kindly to the leading business men of his adopted country, he got hold of Jan Huygen and decided to try his luck in a great gamble. He interested several of the minor capitalists of Enkhuizen, and on the fifth of June of the year 1594 Jan Huygen went upon his first polar exploration with two ships, the Mercurius and the Lwaan. Without adventure the ships passed the North Cape, sailed along the coast of the Kola peninsula, where Willoughby had wintered just forty years before, and reached the Straits of Waigat, the prospective Gibraltar of Dutch aspirations. The conditions of the ice were favorable.

On the first of August of the year 1594 the two ships entered the Kara Sea, which they called the New North Sea. Then following the coast, they entered Kara Bay. After a few days Jan Huygen discovered the small Kara River, the present frontier between Russia and Siberia. He mistook it for the Obi River, and thought that he had gone sufficiently eastward to be certain of the practicability of the new route which he had set out to discover. The ice had all melted. As far as he could see there was open water. He cruised about in this region for several weeks, discovered a number of little islands, and sprinkled the names of all his friends and his employers upon capes and rivers and mountains. Finally, contented with what had been accomplished, he returned home. On the sixteenth of September of the same year he came back to the roads of Texel.

After that he was regarded as the leader in all matters of navigation. The stadholder, Prince Maurice, who had succeeded his father William after the latter had been murdered by one of King Philip's gunmen, sent for Jan Huygen to come to The Hague and report in person upon his discoveries. John of Barneveldt, the clever manager of all the financial and political interests of the republic, discussed with him the possibility of a successful northeastern trading company. Before another year was over Jan Huygen, this time at the head of a fleet of seven ships, was sent northward for a second voyage. Everybody, from his Highness the stadholder down to the speculator who had risked his last pennies, had the greatest expectations. Nothing came of this expedition. As a matter of fact, Jan Huygen had met with exceptionally favorable weather conditions upon his first voyage; on the second he came in for the customary storms and blizzards. His ships were frozen in the ice, and for weeks they could not move. Scurvy attacked the crew and many men died.

In October of the same year he was back in Holland. The only result of the costly expedition was a dead whale that the captain had towed home as an exhibit of his good intentions. He was still a young man, not more than forty-five, but he had had his share of adventures. He did not join the third trip to the North in the next year, about which we shall give a detailed account in our next chapter. He was appointed treasurer of his native city. There he lived as its most respected citizen until the year 1611, when he died and was buried with great solemnity. His work had been done.

In the year 1595 the "Itinerary of His Voyage to the East Indies" had been published. By this book he will always be remembered. For a century it provided a practical handbook of navigation which guided the Dutch traders to the Indies, allowed them to attack the Spaniards and Portuguese in their most vulnerable spot, and gave them the opportunity to found a colonial empire which has lasted to this very day.

CHAPTER II
THE NORTHEAST PASSAGE

Amsterdam, the capital of the new Dutch commonwealth, the rich city which alone counted more people within her wide walls than all of the country provinces put together, had ever been the leader in all matters which offered the chance of an honest penny. Her intellectual glory was a reflected one, her artistic fame was imported from elsewhere; but her exchange dictated its own terms to the rest of the country and to the rest of the world. When the Estates of the Republic gave up the hope of finding the route to India through the frozen Arctic Ocean, Amsterdam had the courage of her nautical convictions, and at her own expense she equipped a last expedition to proceed northward and discover this famous route, which had the advantage of being short and safe.

Out of this expedition grew the famous voyage of Barendsz and Heemskerk to Nova Zembla, the first polar expedition of which we possess a precise account. There were two ships. They were small vessels, for no one wished to risk a large investment on an expedition to the dangerous region of ice and snow. Fewer than fifty men took part, and all had been selected with great care. Married men were not taken; for this expedition might last many years, and it must not be spoiled by the homesick discontent of fathers of families.

Jan Corneliszoon de Ryp was captain of the smaller vessel. The other one was commanded by Jacob van Heemskerk, a remarkable man, an able sailor who belonged to an excellent family and entered the merchant marine at a time when the sea was reserved for those who left shore for the benefit of civic peace and sobriety. He had enjoyed a good education, knew something about scientific matters, and had been in the Arctic a year before with the last and unfortunate expedition of Linschoten. The real leader of this expedition, however, was a very simple fellow, a pilot by the name of Willem, the son of Barend (Barendsz, as it is written in Dutch). He was born on the island of Terschelling and had been familiar with winds and tides since early childhood. Barendsz had two Northern expeditions to his credit, and had seen as much of the coast of Siberia as anybody in the country. A man of great resource and personal courage, combined with a weird ability to guess his approximate whereabouts, he guided the expedition safely through its worst perils. He died in a small open boat in the Arctic Sea. Without his devoted services none of the men who were with him would ever have seen his country again.

There was one other member of the ship's staff who must be mentioned before the story of the trip itself is told. That was the ship's doctor. Officially he was known as the ship's barber, for the professions of cutting whiskers and bleeding people were combined in those happy days. De Veer was a versatile character. He played the flute, organized amateur theatrical performances, kept everybody happy, and finally he wrote the itinerary of the trip, of which we shall translate the most important part.

From former expeditions the sailors had learned what to take with them and what to leave at home. Unfortunately, contractors, then as now, were apt to be scoundrels, and the provisions were not up to the specifications. During the long night of the Arctic winter men's lives depended upon the biscuits that had been ordered in Amsterdam, and these were found to be lacking in both quality and quantity. There were more complaints of the same nature. As the leaders of the expedition fully expected to reach China, they took a fair-sized cargo of trading material, so that the Hollanders might have something to offer the heathen Chinee in exchange for the riches of paradise which this distant and mysterious land was said to possess. On the eighteenth of May everything was ready. Without any difficulty the Arctic Circle was soon reached and passed. Then the trouble began. When two Dutch sailors of great ability and equal stubbornness disagree about points of the compass there is little chance for an agreement. The astronomical instruments of that day allowed certain calculations, but in a rather restricted field. As long as land was near it was possible to sail with a certain degree of precision, but when they were far away from any solid indications of charted islands and continent the captains of that day were often completely at a loss as to their exact whereabouts.

The reason why two of the previous expeditions had failed was known: the ships had been driven into a blind alley called the Kara Sea. In order to avoid a repetition of that occurrence it was deemed necessary to try a more northern course. Barendsz, however, wanted to go due northeast, while De Ryp favored a course more to the west. For the moment the two captains compromised and stayed together. On the fifth of June the sailor on watch in the crow's-nest called out that he saw a lot of swans. The swans were soon found to be ice, the first that was seen that year.

Four days later a new island was discovered. Barendsz thought it must be part of Greenland. After all, he argued, he had been right; the ships had been driven too far westward. De Ryp denied this, and his calculation proved to be true. The ships were still far away from Greenland. The islands belonged to the Spitzbergen Archipelago. On the nineteenth of June they discovered Spitzbergen. The name (steep mountains) describes the island. An expedition was sent ashore, after which we get the first recital of one of the endless fights with bears that greatly frightened the good people in those days of blunderbusses. Nowadays polar bears, while still far removed from harmless kittens, offer no grave danger to modern guns. But the bullets of the small cannon which four centuries ago did service as a rifle refused to penetrate the thick hide of a polar bear. The pictures of De Veer's book indicate that these hungry mammals were not destroyed until they had been attacked by half a dozen men with gunpowder, axes, spears, and meat-choppers.

A very interesting discovery was made on this new island. Every winter wild geese came to the Dutch island of the North Sea. Four centuries ago they were the subject of vague ornithological speculations, for, according to the best authorities of the day, these geese did not behave like chickens and other fowl, which brought up their families out of a corresponding number of eggs. No, their chicks grew upon regular trees in the form of wild nuts. After a while these nuts tumbled into the sea and then became geese. Barendsz killed some of the birds and he also opened their eggs. There were the young chicks! The old myth was destroyed. "But," as he pleasantly remarked, "it is not our fault that we have not known this before, when these birds insist upon breeding so far northward."

On the twenty-fifth of June, Spitzbergen was left behind, and once more a dispute broke out between the two skippers over the old question of the course which was to be taken. Like good Dutchmen, they decided that each should go his own way. De Ryp preferred to try his luck farther to the north. Barendsz and Heemskerk decided to go southward. They said farewell to their comrades, and on the seventeenth of July reached the coast of Nova Zembla. The coast of the island was still little known; therefore the usual expediency of that day was followed. They kept close to the land and sailed until at last they should find some channel that would allow them to pass through into the next sea. They discovered no channel, but on the sixth of August the northern point of Nova Zembla, Cape Nassau, was reached. There was a great deal of ice, but after a few days open water appeared.

The voyage was then continued. Their course then seemed easy. Following the eastern coast downward they were bound to reach the Strait of Kara. Avoiding the Kara Sea, they made for the river Obi and hoped that all would be well. But before the ship had gone many days the cold weather of winter set in, and before the end of August the ship was solidly frozen into the ice. Many attempts were made to dig it out and push it into the open water. The men worked desperately; but the moment they had sawed a channel through the heavy ice to the open sea more ice-fields appeared, and they had to begin all over again. On the thirtieth of August a particularly heavy frost finally lifted the little wooden ship clear out of the ice. Then came a few days of thaw, during which they hoped to get the vessel back into shape and into the water. But the next night there was a repetition of the terrible creakings. The ship groaned as if it were in great agony, and all the men rushed on shore.

The prospect of spending the winter in this desolate spot began to be more than an unspoken fear. Any night the vessel might be destroyed by the violent pressure of the ice. An experienced captain knew what to do in such circumstances. All provisions were taken on shore, and the lifeboats were safely placed on the dry land. They would be necessary the next summer to reach the continent. Another week passed, and the situation was as uncertain as before. By the middle of September, however, all hope had to be given up. The expedition was condemned to spend the winter in the Arctic. The ship's carpenter became a man of importance. Near the small bay into which the vessel had been driven he found a favorable spot for a house. A little river near by provided fresh water. On the whole it was an advantageous spot for shipwrecked sailors, for a short distance towards the north there was a low promontory. The western winds had carried heavy trees and pieces of wood from the Siberian coast, and this promontory had caught them. They were neatly frozen in the ice. All the men needed to do was to take these trees out of their cold storage and drag them ashore which, however, did not prove to be so easy a task as it sounds. There were only seventeen men on the ship, and two of them were too ill to do any work. The others were not familiar with the problem of how to saw and plane water-soaked and frozen logs into planks. Even when this had been done the wood must be hauled a considerable distance on home-made sleighs, clumsy affairs, and very heavy on the soft snow of the early winter.

Unfortunately, after two weeks the carpenter of the expedition suddenly died. It was not easy to give him decent Christian burial. The ground was frozen so hard that spades and axes could not dig a grave; so the carpenter was reverently laid away in a small hollow cut in the solid ice and covered with snow.

When their house was finished it did not offer many of the comforts of home, but it was a shelter against the ever-increasing cold. The roof offered the greatest difficulty to the inexperienced builders. At last they hit upon a scheme that proved successful: they made a wooden framework across which they stretched one of the ship's sails. This they covered with a layer of sand. Then the good Lord deposited a thick coat of snow, which gradually froze and finally made an excellent cover for the small wooden cabin which was solemnly baptized "Safe Haven." There were no windows—fresh air had not yet been invented—and what was the use of windows after the sun had once disappeared? There was one door, and a hole in the roof served as a chimney. To make a better draft for the fire of driftwood which was kept burning day and night in the middle of the cabin floor, a large empty barrel was used for a smoke-stack. Even then the room was full of smoke during all the many months of involuntary imprisonment, and upon one occasion the lack of ventilation almost killed the entire expedition.

While they were at work upon the house the men still spent the night on board their ship. When morning came, with their axes and saws and planes they walked over to the house. But hardly a day went by without a disturbing visit from the much-dreaded polar bears. After some of the provisions had been removed from the ship to the house the bears became more insistent than ever. Upon one occasion when the bears had gone after a barrel of pickled meat, as shown with touching accuracy in the picture, the concerted action of three sailors was necessary to save the food from the savage beasts. Another time, when Heemskerk, De Veer, and one of the sailors were loading provisions upon a sleigh they were suddenly attacked by three huge bears. They had not brought their guns, but they had two halberds, with which they hit the foremost bear upon the snout; and then they fled to the ship and climbed on board. The bears followed, sat down patiently, and laid siege to the ship. The three men on board were helpless. Finally one of them hit upon the idea of throwing a stick of kindling-wood at the bears. Like a well-trained dog, the animal that was struck chased the stick, played with it, and then came back to ask for further entertainment. At last all the kindling-wood laid strewn across the ice, and the bears had had enough of this sport. They made ready to storm the ship, but a lucky stroke with a halberd hit one of them so severely upon the sensitive tip of his nose that he turned around and fled. The others followed, and Heemskerk and his companions were saved.

When the month of November came and the sun had disappeared, the bears also took their departure, rolled themselves up under some comfortable shelter, and went to sleep for the rest of the winter. Now the sailors could wander about in peace, for the only other animal that kept awake all through the year was the polar fox. He was a shy beastie and never came near a human being. The sailors, however, hunted him as best they could. Not only did they need the skins for their winter garments, but stewed fox tasted remarkably like the domestic rabbit and was an agreeable change from the dreary diet of salt-flesh. In Holland before the introduction of firearms rabbits were caught with a net. The same method was tried on Nova Zembla with the more subtle fox. Unfamiliar with the wiles of man, he actually allowed himself to be caught quite easily. Later on traps were also built. But the method with the net was more popular, for the men had the greatest aversion to the fresh air of the freezing polar night and never left the house unless they were ordered to do some work. When they went hunting with the net they could pass the string that dropped the mechanism right under the door and stay inside, where it was warm and cheerful, and yet catch their fox.

On the sixth of November the sun was seen for the last time. On the seventh, when it was quite dark, the clock stopped suddenly in the middle of the night, and when the men got up in the morning they had lost the exact time. For the rest of the winter they were obliged to guess at the approximate hour; not that it mattered so very much, for life had become an endless night: one went to bed and got up through the force of habit acquired by thousands of previous generations. If the men had not been obliged to, they never would have left their comfortable beds. They had but one idea, to keep warm. The complaint about the insufferable cold is the main motive in this Arctic symphony. Lack of regular exercise was chiefly to blame for this "freezing feeling"—lack of exercise and the proper underwear. It is true that the men dressed in many layers of heavy skins, but their lower garments, which nowadays play a great part in the life of modern explorers, were sadly neglected. In the beginning they washed their shirts regularly, but they found it impossible to dry them; for just as soon as the shirt was taken out of the hot water it froze stiff. When they carried the frozen garment into the house to thaw it out before the fire it was either singed and burned in spots or it refused absolutely to melt back into the shape and aspect of a proper shirt. Finally the washing was given up, as it has been on many an expedition, for cleanliness is a costly and complicated luxury when one is away from the beaten track of civilization.

The walls of the house had been tarred and calked like a ship. All the same, when the first blizzards occurred, the snow blew through many cracks, and every morning the men were covered with a coat of snow and ice. Hot-water bottles had not yet been invented, but at night large stones were roasted in the fire until they were hot, and then were placed in the bunks between the fur covers. They helped to keep the men warm, and incidentally they burned their toes before they knew it. Not only did the men suffer in this way. That same clock which I have already mentioned at last succumbed to the strain of alternating spells of heat and cold. It began to go slower and slower. To keep it going at all, the weight was increased every few days. At last, however, a millstone could not have coaxed another second out of the poor mechanism. From that moment on an hour-glass was used. One of the men had to watch it, and turn it over every sixty minutes.

All this time, while the men never ceased their complaint about feeling cold, the heating problem had been solved by fires made of such kindling-wood as the thoughtful ocean had carried across from the Siberian coast and deposited upon the shore. Finally, however, in despair at ever feeling really warm again, if only for a short while, it was decided, as an extra treat, to have a coal fire. There was some coal on board the ship, but it had been saved for use upon the homeward trip in the spring, when the men would be obliged to travel in open boats. The coal was brought to the house. The worst cracks in the walls were carefully filled with tar and rope, and somebody climbed to the roof and closed the chimney; not an ounce of the valuable heat must be lost. As a result the men felt comfortable for the first time in many months; they also came very near losing their lives. Having dozed off in the pleasant heat they had not noticed that their cabin was filling with coal-gas until finally some of them, feeling uncomfortable, tried to get up, grew dizzy, and fainted. Our friend the barber, possessed of more strength than any of the others, managed to creep to the door. He kicked it open and let in the fresh air. The men were soon revived, and the captain treated them all to a glass of wine to celebrate the happy escape. No further experiments with coal were made during that year.

December was a month of steady blizzards. The snow outside piled up in huge drifts which soon reached to the roof. The hungry foxes, attracted by the smell of cookery wafted abroad through the barrel-chimney, used to gallop across the roof, and at night their dismal and mean little bark kept the men in their bunks awake. At the same time their close proximity made trapping easier, and the skins were now doubly welcome; for the shoes, bought in Holland, had been frozen so often and had been thawed out too near the fire so frequently that they were leaking like sieves and could no longer be worn. New shoes were cut out of wood and covered with fox-fur. They provided comfortable, though far from elegant, footwear.

New Year's day was a dreary feast, for all the men thought of home and were melancholy and sad. Outside a terrible snow-storm raged. It continued for an entire week. No one dared to go outside to gather wood, fearing the wind and cold would kill them. In this extremity they were obliged to burn some of their home-made furniture. On the fifth of January the blizzard stopped. The door was opened, the cabin was put in order, wood was brought from the woodpile, and then one of the men suddenly remembered the date and how at home the feast of the Magi was being celebrated with many happy and innocent pastimes. The barber decided to organize a little feast. The first officer was elected to be "King of Nova Zembla." He was crowned with due solemnity. A special dinner of hot pancakes and rusks soaked in wine was served, and the evening was such a success that many imagined themselves safely home in their beloved fatherland. A new blizzard reminded them that they were still citizens of an Arctic island.

On the sixteenth of January, however, the men who had been sent out to look after the traps and bring in wood suddenly noticed a glimmer of red on the horizon. It was a sign of the returning sun. The dreary months of imprisonment were almost over. From that moment the heating problem became less difficult. On the contrary, the roof and the walls now began to leak, and the expedition had its first taste of the thaw which would be even more fatal than the cold weather had proved to be. As has been remarked, these men had been leading a very unhealthy life. While it was still light outside they had sometimes played ball with the wooden knob of the flagpole of the ship, but since early November they had taken no exercise of any sort. A few minutes spent out of doors just long enough to kill the foxes in the traps was all the fresh air they ever got. Out of a barrel they had made themselves a bath-tub, and once a week every man in turn had climbed through the little square opening into that barrel (see the picture) to get steamed out. But this mode of living, combined with bad food, brought half a year before from Holland, together with the large quantity of fox-meat, now caused a great deal of scurvy, and the scurvy caused more dangerous illness. Barendsz, the man upon whom they depended to find the way home, was already so weak that he could not move. He was kept near the fire on a pile of bearskins. On the twenty-sixth of January another man who had been ill for some time suddenly died. His comrades had done all they could to save him. They had cheered him with stories of home, but shortly after midnight of that day he gave up the ghost. Early the next morning he was buried near the carpenter. A chapter of the Bible was read, a psalm was sung, and his sorrowful companions went home to eat breakfast.

None of the men were quite as strong as they had been. Among other things, they hated the eternal bother of keeping the entrance to the door clear of snow. Why should they not abolish the door, and like good Eskimos enter and leave their dwelling-place through the chimney? Heemskerk wanted to try this new scheme and he got ready to push himself through the narrow barrel. At the same time one of the men rushed to the door to go out into the open and welcome the skipper when he should stick his head through the barrel; but before he espied the eminent leader of the expedition he was struck by another sight: the sun had appeared above the horizon. Apparently Barendsz, who had tried to figure out the day and week of the year after they had lost count of the calendar, had been wrong in his calculation. According to him, there were to be two weeks more of darkness. And now, behold! there was the shining orb, speedily followed by a matutinal bear. The lean animal was at once killed and used to replenish the oil of the odorous little lamp which for more than three months had provided the only light inside the cabin.

February came and went, but as yet there were no signs of the breaking up of the ice. During the first day of March a little open water was seen in the distance, but it was too far away to be of any value to the ship. An attempt was made to push the ship out of its heavy coat of ice, but the men at once complained that they were too weak to do much work. Some of them had had their toes frozen and could not walk. Others suffered from frost-bite on their hands and fingers and were unable to hold an ax. When they went outside only incessant vigilance saved them from the claws of the skinny bears that were ready to make up for the long winter's fast. Once a bear almost ate the commander, who was just able to jump inside the house and slam the door on bruin's nose. Another time a bear climbed on the roof, and when he could not get into the chimney, he got hold of the barrel and rocked that architectural contrivance until he almost ruined the entire house. It was very spooky, for the attack took place in the middle of the night, and it was impossible to go out and shoot the monster.

March passed, and the ship, which had been seventy yards away from the water when it was deserted in the autumn of 1595, was now more than five hundred yards away from the open sea. The intervening distance was a huge mass of broken ice and snow-drifts. It seemed impossible to drag the boats quite so far. When on the first of May the last morsel of salt meat had been eaten, the men appeared to be as far away from salvation as ever. There was a general demand that something be done. They had had enough of one winter in the Arctic, and would rather risk a voyage in an open boat than another six months of cold bunks and tough fox-stew, and reading their Bible by the light of a single oil-lamp.

Fortunately—and this is a great compliment to a dozen men who have been cooped up in a small cabin for six months of dark and cold—the spirit of the sailors had been excellent, and discipline had been well maintained. They did not make any direct demands upon the captain. The question of going or staying they discussed first of all with the sick Barendsz, and he in turn mentioned it to Heemskerk. Heemskerk himself was in favor of waiting a short while. He reasoned that the ice might melt soon, and then the ship could be saved. He, as captain, was responsible for his craft. He asked that they wait two weeks more. If the condition of the ice was still unsatisfactory at the end of that time, they would give up the ship and try to reach home in the boats. Meanwhile the men could get ready for the trip. They set to work at once cleaning and repairing their fur coats, sharpening their tools, and covering their shoes with new skins to keep their feet from freezing during the long weeks in the open boats.

An eastern storm on the last day of May filled their little harbor with more ice, and all hope of saving the ship was given up. The return trip must be made in the open boats. There were two, a large and a small one. They had been left on land in the autumn, and were now covered with many feet of frozen snow. A first attempt to dig them out failed. The men were so weak that they could not handle their axes and spades. The inevitable bear attacked them, drove them post-haste back to the safe shelter of the house, and so put an end to the first day's work.

The next morning the men went back to their work. Regular exercise and fresh air soon gave them greater strength, while the dire warning of Heemskerk that, unless they succeeded, they would be obliged to end their days as citizens of Nova Zembla provided an excellent spur to their digging enthusiasm. The two boats were at last dragged to the house to be repaired. They were in very bad condition, but since there was no further reason for saving the ship there was sufficient wood with which to make good the damage. From early to late the men worked, the only interruptions being the dinner-hour and the visits of the bears. "But," as De Veer remarked in his pleasant way, "these animals probably knew that we were to leave very soon, and they wanted to have a taste of us before we should have gone for good." Before that happy hour arrived the expedition was threatened with a novel, but painful, visitation. To vary the monotonous diet of bearsteak, the men had fried the liver. Three of them had eaten of this dish and fell so ill that all hope was given up of saving their lives. The others, who knew that they could not handle the boats if three more sailors were to die, waited in great anxiety. Fortunately on the fourth day the patients showed signs of improvement and finally recovered. There were no further experiments with scrambled bear's liver.

After that the work on the two boats proceeded with speed, and by the twelfth of June everything was ready. The boats, now reinforced for the long trip across the open water of the Arctic Ocean, had to be hauled to the sea, and the ever-shifting wind had once more put a high ice-bank between the open water and the shore. A channel was cut through the ice with great difficulty, for there were no tools for this work. After two days more the survivors of this memorable shipwreck were ready for the last part of their voyage. Before they left the house Barendsz wrote three letters in which he recounted the adventures of the expedition. One of these letters was placed in a powder-horn which was left hanging in the chimney, where it was found two hundred and fifty years later.

On the morning of the fourteenth, Barendsz and another sick sailor who could no longer walk were carried to the boats. With a favorable wind from the south they set sail for the northern cape of Nova Zembla, which was soon reached. Then they turned westward, and followed the coast until they should reach the Siberian continent. The voyage along the coast was both difficult and dangerous. The two boats were not quite as large as the life-boats of a modern liner. Being still too weak to row, the men were obliged to sail between huge icebergs, often being caught for hours in the midst of large ice-fields. Sometimes they had to drag the boats upon the ice while they hacked a channel to open water. After a week the condition of the ice forced them to pull the boats on shore and wait for several days before they could go any farther. Great and tender care was taken of the sick pilot and the dying sailor, but those nights spent in the open were hard on the sufferers. On the morning of the twentieth of June the sailor, whose name was Claes Andriesz, felt that his end was near. Barendsz, too, said he feared that he would not last much longer. His active mind kept at work until the last. De Veer, the barber, had drawn a map of the coast, and Barendsz offered suggestions. Capes and small islands off the coast were definitely located, placed in their correct geographical positions, and baptized with sound Dutch names.

The end of Barendsz came very suddenly. Without a word of warning he turned his eyes toward heaven, sighed, and fell back dead. A few hours later he was followed by the faithful Claes. They were buried together. Sad at heart, the survivors now risked their lives upon the open sea. They had all the adventures not uncommon to such an expedition. The boats were in a rotten condition; several times the masts broke, and most of the time the smaller boat was half full of water. The moment they reached land and tried to get some rest, there was a general attack by wild bears. And once a sudden break in a field of ice separated the boats from the provisions, which had just been unloaded. In their attempt to get these back several men broke through the ice. They caught cold, and on the fifth of July another sailor, a relative of Claes, who had died with Barendsz, had to be buried on shore.

During all this misery we read of a fine example of faithful performance of duty and of devotion to the interest of one's employers. You will remember that this expedition had been sent out to reach China by the Northeast Passage and to establish commercial relations with the merchants of the great heathen kingdom. For this purpose rich velvets and other materials agreeable to the eyes of Chinamen had been loaded onto the ship when they left Amsterdam. Heemskerk felt it his duty to save these goods, and he had managed to keep them in safety. Now that the sun shone with some warmth, the packages were opened and their contents dried. When Heemskerk came back to Amsterdam the materials were returned to their owners in good condition.

On the eleventh of June of the year 1597 the boats were approaching the spot where upon previous voyages large colonies of geese had been found. They went ashore and found so many eggs that they did not know how to take them all back to the boats. So two men took down their breeches, tied the lower part together with a piece of string, filled them with eggs, and carried their loot in triumph back to the others on board.

That was almost their last adventure with polar fauna, except for an attack by infuriated seals whose quiet they had disturbed. The seals almost upset one of the boats. The men had no further difficulties, however. On the contrary, from now on everything was plain sailing; and it actually seemed to them that the good Lord himself had taken pity upon them after their long and patient suffering, for whenever they came to a large ice-field it would suddenly separate and make a clear channel for their boats; and when they were hungry they found that the small islands were covered with birds that were so tame that they waited to be caught and killed.

At last, on the twenty-seventh of July, they arrived in open water where they discovered a strong eastern current. They decided that they must be near Kara Strait. The next morning they hoped to find out for certain. When the next morning came they suddenly beheld two strange vessels near their own boats. They were fishing-smacks, to judge by their shape and size, but nothing was known about their nationality, for they flew no flags, and it was well to be careful in the year of grace 1597. Therefore a careful approach was made. To Heemskerk's great joy, the ships were manned by Russians who had seen the fleet of Linschoten several years before and remembered some of the Hollanders. There were familiar faces on both sides, and this first glimpse of human beings did more to revive the courage of the men than the doubtful food which the Russians forced with great hospitality upon their unexpected guests. The following day the two fishing-boats set sail for the west, and Heemskerk followed in their wake. But in the afternoon they sailed into a heavy fog and when it lifted no further trace of the Russians could be found. Once more the two small boats were alone, with lots of water around them and little hope before them.

By this time all of the men had been attacked by scurvy and they could no longer eat hard-tack, which was the only food left on board. Divine interference again saved them. They found a small island covered with scurvy-grass (Cochlearia officinalis) the traditional remedy for this painful affliction. Within a few days they all recovered, and could row across the current of the straits which separated them from the continent. Here they found another Russian ship. Then they discovered that their compass, on account of the proximity of heavy chests and boxes covered with iron rings, had lost all track of the magnetic pole and that they were much farther toward the east than they had supposed. They deliberated whether they should continue their voyage on land or on sea. Finally they decided to stick to their boats and their cargo. Once more they closely followed the coast until they came to the mouth of the White Sea. That meant a vast stretch of dangerous open water, which must be crossed at great risk. The first attempt to reach the other shore failed. The two boats lost sight of each other, and they all worried about the fate of their comrades. On the eighteenth of August the second boat managed to reach the Kola peninsula after rowing for more than thirty hours.

That virtually ends the adventures of the men who had gone out with Barendsz and Heemskerk to discover the Northeast Passage, and who quite involuntarily acted as the first polar explorers. After a few days the boats found each other, and together they reached the first Russian settlement, where they found houses and warm rooms and a chance to get a decent bath and eat from a table. Their misery was at once forgotten. At heart they were healthy-minded, simple fellows, and when for the first time after many months they saw some women they were quite happy, although these women were Laplanders and proverbially lacking in those attributes which we usually connect with the idea of lovely womanhood.

News traveled fast even in the dominion of the Lapp. In less than eighty hours a Laplander came running to the Russian settlement with a letter which had been written by De Ryp, who, half a year before, had been blown into the White Sea and was now waiting for a favorable wind to sail home. He was still in Kola, and was delighted at the safe return of his colleague from whom he had separated over a point of nautical difference. He invited the men to go home with him. The two small boats of Heemskerk's ship were left in the town of Kola as a small souvenir for the kind-hearted Russians, the Arctic costumes were carefully packed away, to be shown to the family at home, and on the sixth of October they all said farewell to the Russian coast. Twenty-three days later they entered the Maas. By way of Maassluis, Delft, The Hague, and Haarlem they made their triumphant entry into Amsterdam. Dressed in their fox-skins and their home-made wooden shoes, they paraded through the streets of the city. Their High and Mightinesses the mayors received them at the town hall, and the world was full of the fame of this first Arctic expedition. As for the practical results, there were none, unless we except the negative information about the impossibility of the Northeastern Passage. But nobody cared any longer about this route, for just two months before the first Dutch fleet which had tried to reach the Indies by way of the Cape had safely returned to the roads of Texel. The Portuguese, after all, had proved to be not so dangerous as had been expected. The Indian native was quite willing to welcome the Dutch trader. And the Northeastern route, after the wonderful failures of a number of conscientious expeditions, was given up for the well-worn and well-known route along the African coast. The Arctic was all right for the purpose of hunting of the profitable whale, but as a short cut to the Indies it had proved an absolute disappointment.

CHAPTER III
THE TRAGEDY OF SPITZBERGEN

Before I tell you the story of the first voyage to India I want to give a short account of another Dutch expedition in the Arctic Sea which ended even more sadly than that of Heemskerk and Barendsz.

On their voyage to Nova Zembla the two mariners had discovered a group of islands which on account of their high mountains they had called the "Islands of the Steep Peaks," or Spitzbergen in the Dutch language. These islands provided an excellent center for the whaling fisheries. During the first half of the seventeenth century a large Dutch fleet went northward every spring to catch whales. The dead animals were brought to Spitzbergen, where the blubber was turned into whale-oil, and the rest of the huge animal was got ready for a market that was not as finicky in its taste as in our own time.

Soon a small city was built around the large furnaces and the rooming-houses for the workmen. This town was appropriately called "Greaseville" (in Dutch, Smeerenburg). It consisted of the usual gathering of saloons, eating-places, and small stores, that you might find in a Western American town during a mining boom. When the autumn came, the inhabitants moved back to Holland and left the city to the tender mercies of the bears and foxes. Unfortunately, the owners of this curious and somewhat motley settlement were not always the first to arrive upon the scene in the summer. Other sailors, Scotch or Norwegian, had often visited Greaseville before they arrived and either appropriated what they wanted or destroyed what they could not carry away. As early as 1626 a plan was discussed of leaving a guard on the island during the winter. The men could live comfortably in one of the houses and they could support themselves by hunting and fishing. It was not a bad idea, but Nova Zembla still spooked in people's heads, and nobody wanted to try a winter of darkness and cold such as had been just described by De Veer. But in the year 1630 eight English sailors were accidentally left behind from a ship, and next spring they were found little the worse for wear. As a result the experiment was at last made in the winter of the year 1633. Seven men were left on Spitzbergen and seven others on the Jan Mayen, an island somewhat to the west and farther away from the pole. The seven on Jan Mayen all died of scurvy. When next spring a fleet came to relieve them they were found frozen dead in their bunks. On Spitzbergen, however, all the men had passed a comfortable winter. They had suffered a good deal from the cold, but they had managed to keep out in the open, take a lot of exercise, and pass the long winter as cheerfully as the heavy blizzards and storms allowed. It was decided to leave a small guard upon the island every year. When in September of 1634 the fleet of whalers sailed back for Holland, seven new men, under the leadership of Adriaen Janzzoon, who came from Delft, had agreed to remain behind and keep watch over the little settlement of Smeerenburg. They were well provided with supplies, but all perished before the spring of the next year. They left a diary, and from this we copy a few items to show the quiet and resigned courage with which they went to their death.

"On the eleventh of September of the year of our Lord 1634 the whaling ships sailed for home. We wished them a happy voyage. We saw several whales and often tried to get one, but we did not succeed. We looked for fresh vegetables, foxes, and bears with great industry, but we did not find any.

"Between the twentieth and the twenty-first of October the sun left us. On the twenty-fourth of November we began to suffer from scurvy. Therefore we looked for fresh vegetables, foxes, and bears with great industry, but we did not succeed, to our great grief. Therefore we consoled each other that the good Lord would provide. On the second of December Klaes Florisz took a remedy against scurvy, and we set traps to catch foxes.

"On the eleventh of December Jeroen Caroen also took a remedy against scurvy, and we all began to eat separately from each other because some suffered more from scurvy and others less. We looked every day, trying to find fresh vegetables, but we found nothing. So we recommended our souls into the hands of God.

"On the twelfth of December Cornelis Thysz took a remedy for scurvy. On the twenty-third of December we saw our first bear. Just as the cook was pouring out hot water from his kitchen the bear stood outside the window, but when he heard a noise he hastily fled. On the twenty-fourth we again heard a bear, and we at once ran for him with three men, whereupon he stood upright on his hind legs and looked quite horrible; but we shot a musket-ball through his belly, and he began to groan and bleed quite badly, and with his teeth he bit one of our halberds to pieces and then fled. We followed him with two lanterns, but we could not get him, although we needed him sorely on account of the sick people as well as of those who were still well, for nobody was quite without pain. If things do not improve before long we shall all be dead before the ships come back; but God knows what is best for us. On the twenty-fifth of December Cornelis Thysz took a remedy for scurvy for the second time, for things were going badly with him. On the fourteenth of January Adriaen Janszoon died, being the first of the seven of us to go; but we are now all very ill and have much pain.

"On the fifteenth Fetje Otjes died.

"On the seventeenth Cornelis Thysz died. Next to God we had put our hope upon him. We who were still alive made coffins for the three dead ones, and we laid them into their coffins, although we were hardly strong enough to do this, and every day we are getting worse.

"On the twenty-eighth we saw the first fox, but we could not get him. On the twenty-ninth we killed our red dog, and we ate him in the evening. On the seventh of February we caught our first fox, and we were all very happy; but it did not do us much good, for we are all too far gone by now. We saw many bears, yes, sometimes we saw as many as three, four, five, six, ten, twelve at the same time; but we did not have strength enough to fire a gun, and even if we had hit a bear, we could not have walked out to get him, for we are all so weak that we can not put one foot before the other. We can not even eat our bread; we have terrible pains all over our bodies; and the worse the weather is the more pain we have. Many of us are losing blood. Jeroan Caroen is the strongest, and he went out and got some coals to make a fire.

"On the twenty-third we laid flat on our backs almost all the time. The end has come, and we commend our souls into the hands of God.

"On the twenty-fourth we saw the sun again, for which we praised God, for we had not seen the sun since the twentieth or twenty-first of October of last year.

"On the sixth of February the four of us who are still alive are lying in our bunks. We would eat something if only one of us were strong enough to get up and make a fire; we can not move from the pain we suffer. With folded hands we pray to God to deliver us from this sorrowful world. If it pleases Him we are ready; for we would prefer not to stand this suffering much longer without food and without a fire, and yet we cannot help each other, and each one must bear his own fate as well as he can."

When the ships came to Spitzbergen in the spring of 1635 they found the cabin locked. A sailor climbed into the house through the attic window. The first things he found were pieces of the red dog hanging from the rafters, where they had been put to dry. In front of the stairs he stumbled over the frozen body of the other dog. Inside the cabin the seven sailors rested together. Three were lying in open coffins, two in one bunk, two others on a piece of sail on the floor, all of them frozen, with their knees pulled up to their chins.

That was the last time an attempt was made to have anybody pass the winter on the island.

CHAPTER IV THE FIRST VOYAGE TO INDIA—FAILURE

It was no mean expedition which set sail for the Indies on the second of April of the year 1595 with four ships, 284 men, and an investment of more than three hundred thousand guilders. Amsterdam merchants had provided the capital and the ships. The Estates of Holland and a number of cities in the same province had sent cannon. With large cannon and small harquebus, sixty-four in number, they were a fair match for any Spaniard or Portuguese who might wish to defend his ancient rights upon this royal Indian route, which ran down the Atlantic, doubled the Cape of Good Hope, and then made a straight line from the southernmost tip of Africa to Cape Comorin on the Indian peninsula in Asia.

A few words should be said about the ships, for each was to experience adventures before reaching the safe harbor of home or disappearing silently in a lonely sea. There were the Hollandia, proudly called after the newly created sovereign republic of the seven united Netherlands; the Mauritius, bearing the name of the eminent general whose scientific strategy was forcing the Spanish intruder from one province after the other; the Amsterdam, the representative of a city which in herself was a mighty commonwealth; and lastly a small and fast ship called the Pigeon.

Also, since there were four ships, there were four captains, and thereby hangs a tale. This new Dutch Republic was a democracy of an unusually jealous variety, which is saying a great deal. Its form of government was organized disorder. The principle of divided power and governmental wheels within wheels at home was maintained in a foreign expedition where a single autocratic head was a most imperative necessity. What happened during the voyage was this: the four captains mutually distrustful, each followed his own obstinate will. They quarreled among themselves, they quarreled with the four civil directors who represented the owners and the capitalists in Holland, and who together with the captains were supposed to form a legislative and executive council for all the daily affairs of the long voyage. Finally they quarreled with the chief representative of the commercial interests, Cornelis de Houtman, a cunning trader and commercial diplomatist who had spent four years in Lisbon trying to discover the secrets of Indian navigation. Indeed, so great had been his zeal to get hold of the information hidden in the heads of Portuguese pilots and the cabalistic meaning of Portuguese charts, that the authorities, distrustful of this too generous foreigner, with his ever-ready purse, had at last clapped him into jail.

Then there had been a busy correspondence with the distant employers of this distinguished foreign gentleman. Amsterdam needed Houtman and his knowledge of the Indian route. The money which in the rotten state of Portugal could open the doors of palaces as well as those of prisons brought the indiscreet pioneer safely back to his fatherland. Now, after another year, he was appointed to be the leading spirit of a powerful small fleet and the honorable chairman of a complicated and unruly council of captains and civilian directors. That is to say, he might have been their real leader if he had possessed the necessary ability; but the task was too much for him. For not only was he obliged to keep the peace between his many subordinate commanders, but he was also obliged to control the collection of most undesirable elements who made up the crews of this memorable expedition. I am sorry that I have to say this, but in the year 1595 people did not venture upon a phantastical voyage to an unknown land along a highly perilous route unless there was some good reason why they should leave their comfortable native shores. The commanders of the ships and their chief officers were first class sailors. The lower grades, too, were filled with a fairly sober crowd of men, but the common sailor almost without exception belonged to a class of worthless youngsters who left their country for their country's good and for the lasting benefit of their family's reputation. There was, however, a saving grace, and we must give the devil his due. Many of these men were desperately brave. When they were well commanded they made admirable sailors and excellent soldiers, but the moment discipline was relaxed, they ran amuck, killed their officers or left them behind on uninhabited islands and lived upon the fat of the commissary department until the last bottle of gin was emptied and the last ham was eaten. In most cases their ship then ran on a hidden cliff, whereupon the democratic sea settled all further troubles with the help of the ever-industrious shark.

When we realize that the Dutch colonial empire was conquered with and by such men we gain a mighty respect for the leaders whose power of will turned these wild bands of adventurers into valiant soldiers. And when we study the history of our early colonial system we no longer wonder that it was so bad. We are gratefully astonished that it was not vastly worse.

On the tenth of March of the year 1595 the crews had been mustered, the last provisions had been taken on board. Everything was ready for the departure. The riot act was read to the men, for discipline was maintained by means of the gallows and the flogging-pole, and after a great deal of gunpowder had been wasted upon salutes the ships sailed to the Texel. Here they waited in the roads for two weeks, and then with a favorable wind from the north set sail for the English Channel. All this and the rest of the story which is to follow we have copied from the diary of Frank van der Does, who was on board the Hollandia and who was one of the few officers who got safely home.

During the first three weeks it was plain sailing. On the twenty-sixth of April the fleet reached one of the Cape Verde Islands. Some of the wild goats of the islands that had so greatly impressed Linschoten were caught and divided among the sailors, making a very welcome change in their eternal diet of salted meat. Another week went by, and two Portuguese freighters, loaded to the gunwales, appeared upon the horizon. Kindly remember that this was only a few years after the desperate struggle with Spain and while yet any ship that might be considered popish was a welcome prize. Therefore the instinct of all the Hollanders on board demanded that this easy booty be captured. These ships, so the men reasoned, would provide more profit than an endless, dreary trip to an unknown Indian sea; but for once discipline prevailed. The commanders were under strict order not to do any freebooting on their own account. On the contrary, they must make friends wherever they could. Accordingly, the Dutch admiral gave the Portuguese a couple of hams, and the Portuguese returned the favor with a few jars of preserved fruit. Then the two squadrons separated, and the Dutch fleet went southward.

In the end of June the ships passed the equator, and scurvy made its customary appearance among the men. The suspicion that scurvy might have something to do with the lack of certain elements in the daily food had begun to dawn upon the sailors of that time. Of course it was quite impossible for them to carry fresh solid food in their little and ill-ventilated ships, but they could take fluids. Water was never drunk by sailors of that day. It spoiled too easily in the primitive tanks. Beer was the customary beverage. This time, however, a large supply of wine had been taken along, and when they reached the tropics each of the sailors got a pint of wine per day as a remedy or, rather, a preventive of the dreaded disease. But it increased rapidly, and with a feeling of deep relief the sailors welcomed the appearance of wild birds, which indicated that the Cape of Good Hope must be near. Early in August they sailed past the southern point of the African continent, and dropped anchor in a small bay near the spot where now the town of Port Elizabeth is situated. Here our friend Van der Does was sent on shore with two boats to find fresh water. His first attempt at a landing did not succeed. The boats got into a very heavy surf. They were attacked by a couple of playful whales, and on the shore excited natives, reputed to be cannibals, danced about in gleeful anticipation. A storm broke loose, and for almost an entire day the men floated helplessly on the angry waves. When at last they returned to the ship the other sailors had already given them up as lost.

The next day the weather was more favorable, and they managed to reach the shore, where they made friends with the natives. According to the description, these must have been Hottentots. They made a very bad impression. The Hottentot, then as now, was smallish and very ugly, with a lot of black hair that looked as if it had been singed. In short, in the language of the sixteenth century they looked like people who had been hanging on the gallows for a long time and had shriveled into the leathern caricature of a man. A dirty piece of skin served them as clothing, and their language sounded to the Dutch sailors like the cackling of a herd of angry turkeys. As for their manners, they were beastly. When they killed an animal, they ate it raw, both insides and outsides. Perhaps they stopped long enough to scrape some of the dirt off with their fingers, but usually they did not take the trouble to cook their food. Furthermore—this, however, so far was only a suspicion—they were said to be cannibals and ate their own kind.

The happy Hottentot still lived in the Stone Age, and these first European traders were a veritable godsend to a people obliged to hunt with stone arrows. The expedition did not fail to discover this, and for a few knives and a few simple iron objects they received all the cows and sheep they wanted. And, to our great joy, we get our first glimpse of that most amusing and clownish of all living creatures, the penguin. The penguin has risen in the social scale of wild birds since he has become one of the chief attractions of the moving-pictures. In the year 1595 he was every bit as silly and absurd an animal as he is now, when he wanders forth to make friends with the sailors of our South Polar expeditions. Van der Does hardly knew what to make of this strange creature which has wings, yet cannot fly, and whose feathers look like the smooth skin of a seal. Strangest of all, this wild animal was found to be so tame that the sailors had to box their ears before they could force a narrow path through the dense crowds of excited birds.

On the eleventh of August the ships left the safe harbor. Their original plan had been to cross the Indian Ocean from this point and to make directly for the Indian islands, but there had been so much illness among the crew that the plan had to be given up. They decided to call at Madagascar first of all. There they hoped to find an abundance of fresh fruit and to spend some weeks in which to allow the sick people to recover completely before they ventured, into the actual domains of the Portuguese.

Unfortunately, the navigating methods of that day were still very primitive. A profound trust in the Lord made up for a lack of knowledge of the compass. The good Lord in his infinite mercy usually guided the ship until it reached some shore or other. Then the navigator set to work and wormed his way either upward or downward until at last he struck the spot which he had been trying to reach all the time and thanked divine Providence for his luck. The particular bay renowned for its fresh water and vegetables, that the expedition hoped to reach was situated on the east coast of Madagascar, but a small gale blew the ships to the westward. They could not reach the southern cape, and they were forced to take whatever the western coast could provide. That was little enough. There was an abundance of wild natives. Upon one occasion the natives caught a landing party and stripped them of all their arms and clothes before they allowed them to return to their ships. But there were no wild fruit-trees, and upon these now depended the lives of the members of the expedition.

Seventy sailors were dead. Worst of all, the captain of the Hollandia, Jan Dignumsz by name, the most energetic of the leaders and famous for his discipline, had also died. A small island was used as a cemetery, and was baptized Deadmen's Land, where rested one-quarter of the men who had left Holland. The situation was far from pleasant when the Pigeon, which had been sent out to reconnoiter, came back with good tidings. A tribe of natives had been found that was willing to enter into peaceful trade with the Hollanders and to sell their cattle in exchange for knives and beads. It was almost too good to be true. For a single tin spoon these simple people would give an entire ox or four sheep. A steel knife induced them to offer one of their daughters as a slave.

At this spot the sick people were landed, to be tended on shore. Soon the misery was forgotten in the contemplation of an abundance of wild monkeys, which competed with the natives in the execution of wild and curious dances and which when roasted on hot coals made a fine dish. This idyl, however, did not last long. The "pious life" of the sailors and their attitude toward the natives soon caused considerable friction. One night the natives attacked the camp where the sick men slept. The Hollanders, from their side, took four young natives to their ships and kept them there as prisoners. The four of course tried to escape. One was drowned, pulled down by his heavy chains. Two others hid themselves in a small boat and were recaptured the next day. A few days after this event the mate of one of the ships and another sailor went on shore and tried to buy a cow. They were attacked. The sailor was mortally wounded, and the mate had his throat cut. In revenge the Hollanders shot one of the natives and burned down a few villages. It is a sad story, but we shall often have to tell of this sort of thing when the white man made his first appearance among his fellow-creatures of a different hue.

After this adventure the council of captains decided to proceed upon the voyage without further delay. On the thirteenth of December the fleet started upon the last stretch of water which separated it from the island of Java. After two weeks, however, scurvy once more played such havoc among the sailors that the ships were obliged to sail back to Madagascar. They found the small island called *Santa Maria* on the east coast. The natives here were more civilized, there was an abundance of fresh food, and the sick people recovered in a short time. Except for a sufficient supply of water, the expedition was ready for the last thousand miles across the Indian Ocean. *Santa Maria*, however, did not provide enough water.

Once more a sloop was sent out to reconnoiter. In the Bay of Saint Antongil, on the main island, they discovered a small river, and on the twenty-fifth of January the four ships reached this bay. They started filling their water-kegs when on the third of February a terrible storm drove the Hollandia on a shoal and almost wrecked the ship. During the attempts at getting her afloat two of her boats were swept away and were washed on shore. The next morning a sloop was sent after these boats, but during the night the natives, in their desire for iron nails, had hacked the boats to pieces. When thereupon the boat with sailors approached the village, the natives, expecting a punitive expedition, attacked the men with stones. The Hollanders fired their muskets, the power of which seemed unknown to these people, for they gazed at the murderous arms with great curiosity until a number of them had been killed, when they ran away and hid themselves. After the fashion of that day the

Dutch crew then burned down a few hundred native huts. Such was the end of the first visit of Hollanders to Madagascar. On the thirteenth of February the ships left for the Indies, but before they got so far the long-expected internal disorder had broken loose.

I have mentioned that the captain of the Hollandia had died on the west coast of Madagascar. The owners of the ships, not wishing to leave anything to luck, had provided each ship with sealed instruction, telling the officers who should succeed whom in case of just such an accident. These letters were to be opened in the full council of captains. Instead of doing this, the civil commissioner on the Hollandia had opened his letter at once and had read therein that the office of captain should be bestowed upon the first mate, De Keyser by name, and a personal friend of the commissioner. It is difficult at this late date to discover what caused all the trouble which followed. De Keyser was a good man, the most popular officer of the fleet, while Houtman, the civilian commander of the expedition, was very much disliked by the officers of all the ships. There is nothing very peculiar in this. Civilians are never wanted on board a fleet, least of all when they have been sent out to control the actions of the regular seafaring people. It is not surprising, therefore, to find the officers taking the side of De Keyser and turning against the civilians. Houtman in his high official altitude and in a very tactless way, declared that he would not recognize De Keyser. De Keyser, to avoid friction, then declared that he would voluntarily resign, but the other officers declared that they would not hear of such a thing. Thereupon Houtman insisted that he, as civilian commander, had a right to demand the strictest obedience to the orders of the owners. The officers told Houtman what they would be before they obeyed a mere civilian. Houtman stood his ground. The council of the captains broke up in a free-for-all fight, and the most violent backers of De Keyser declared that they would shoot Houtman rather than give in. Thus far the quarrel had been about the theoretical principle whether the actual sailors or the civilian commissioners should be the masters of the fleet. But when the man who had started the whole trouble by opening the sealed letter against orders proposed to desert the fleet with the Hollandia he committed a breach of etiquette which at once made him lose the support of the other regular officers. Discipline was discipline.

The mutineer was brought before a court-martial and was ordered to be put in irons until the end of the voyage. He actually made the remainder of the trip as a prisoner. The suit against him was not dropped until after the return to Holland. It was a storm in a tea-kettle, or, rather, it was a quarrel between a few dozen people, most of them ill, who were cooped up in four small and ill-smelling vessels and who had got terribly on one another's nerves. It is needless to say that these official disagreements greatly entertained the rough elements in the forecastle, who witnessed this commotion with hidden glee and decided that they would have some similar fun of their own as soon as possible.

Meanwhile the wind had been favorable, and on the fifth of June, after a long, but uneventful voyage, an island was seen. It proved to be a small island off the coast of Sumatra. Sumatra itself was reached two days later, and on the eleventh of the same month the Sunda Archipelago, between Sumatra and Java, was reached. In this part of the Indies the white man had been before. The natives, therefore, knew the power of firearms, and they were accordingly cautious. One of them who was familiar with the straits between the islands offered to act as pilot on their further trip to Bantam. For eight reals in gold he promised to guide them safely to the north shore of Java. The amount was small, but the distance was short. On the twenty-third of June of the year 1596 four Dutch ships appeared for the first time in the roads of Bantam, and were welcomed by the Portuguese with all the civility which the sight of sixty-four cannon demanded. At that time Bantam was an important city, the most important trading center of the western part of the Indian islands. It was the capital of a Mohammedan sultan, and for many years it had been the residence of a large Portuguese colony. Besides Javanese natives and Portuguese settlers there were many Arab traders and Chinese merchants. All of these hastened forth to inspect the ships with the strange flag and have a look at this new delegation of white men who were blond, not dark like the Portuguese, and who spoke an unknown language.

The fleet had now reached its destination, and the actual work of the commercial delegates began. It was their business to conclude an official treaty with the native authorities and to try to obtain equal trading rights with the Portuguese. Houtman was of great value in this sort of negotiation. As representative of the mighty Prince Maurice of Nassau, who for the benefit of the natives was described as the most high potentate of the most powerful Dutch commonwealth, he called upon the regent, who was governing the country during the minority of the actual sultan. He made his visit in great state, and through a number of presents he gained the favor of the regent. On the first of July he obtained the desired commercial treaty. The Hollanders were allowed to trade freely, and a house was put at their disposal to serve as a general office and storeroom. Two of the civilian directors were allowed to live on shore, and everything was ready for business. Thus far things had gone so well that Houtman decided to perform his task leisurely. The new pepper harvest was soon to be gathered, and he thought it well to wait until he had a chance to get fresh spices. What was left of last year's crop was offered for a very low price, but as there was no hurry, no supply was bought.

Unfortunately, this time of waiting was utilized

by the Portuguese for a campaign of underhand agitation against their unwelcome rivals. They did not accuse the Hollanders directly of any evil intentions, but did the regent know who those people were? It is true that they claimed to be the representatives of a certain Prince of Nassau. Was there such a Prince? They might just as well be common buccaneers. It would be much safer if the regent would order his soldiers to take all the Hollander people prisoner and to surrender them to the Portuguese, to be dealt with according to their deserts.

The regent, who knew nothing about his new guests except that they were white and had come to him in wooden ships, listened with an attentive ear. At first he did not act, but the Hollanders soon noticed that whereas they found it difficult to buy anything at all in Bantam, Portuguese vessels left the harbor every week with heavy cargoes. At last when the commissary department of the Dutch fleet sent on shore for provisions they were refused all further supplies. Evidently something was going to happen.

To be well prepared against all eventualities, the Dutch captains began to chart the harbor. With the small guns of that age it was necessary to know exactly how near shore one could get in order to bombard the enemy. The natives saw the manœuvering, and wondered what it was all about. From that moment on there was suspicion on both sides, and at last the tension between them grew so serious that the Hollanders decided to remove their goods from their storehouse and bring them on the ships. But while they were loading their possessions into the boats Houtman and another civilian by the name of Willem Lodewycksz were suddenly taken prisoner and brought to the castle of the regent. This dignitary, afraid of the Portuguese, whose power he appreciated, and yet unwilling to act openly against some newcomers who might be far more dangerous, wanted to keep the leader of the Dutch expedition and one of his officers as hostages until the Dutch ships should have left the port without doing him or his people any harm.

The Hollanders, however, who knew that the Portuguese were responsible for this action, at once attacked the Portuguese ships. Both parties, however, proved to be equally strong, and having fired several volleys at one another, both sides gave up their quarrel and waited until they should be reinforced. Houtman and his companion were set free after the Hollanders had paid a heavy ransom. All this took place in the month of October. Even then Houtman hoped that the interrupted trading might be resumed. Meanwhile, however, the Portuguese had asked for reinforcements to be sent from their colony in Malacca, and a high Portuguese official was already on his way to Bantam to offer the regent ten thousand reals for the surrender of the entire Dutch fleet. Of these negotiations the Dutch commander obtained full details through a friendly Portuguese merchant. Since everybody spied upon everybody else, this merchant's secret correspondence was soon detected, and the culprit was sent to Malacca. As there was now no longer any hope for profitable business, the Dutch fleet made ready to depart. Just before leaving, however, they managed to get some cargo. A Chinaman got on board the admiral's ship, and made him the following offer. He would load two vessels with spices and would leave the port. The Hollanders would attack his vessels and would capture both ship and cargo. Of course they must pay cash and must deposit the money beforehand.

This was done, and in this way Houtman got several thousand guilders' worth of nutmeg and mace. Thereupon the Hollanders left

Bantam and tried their luck in several other cities on the Javanese coast; but everywhere the people had been warned by the Portuguese against ungodly pirates who were soon to come with four big ships, and everywhere the ships were refused water and were threatened with open hostilities if they should attempt to buy anything from the natives.

One little king, however, appeared to have more friendly feelings. That was the King of Sidayu, on the strait of Surabaya. He was very obliging indeed, and volunteered to pay the first call upon his distinguished visitors. At the hour which had been officially announced his Majesty, with a large number of well-armed canoes, paddled out to the Dutch ships. The Hollanders, glad at last to find so cheerful a welcome, had arranged everything for a festive occasion. The ships had hoisted their best array of flags, and the trumpeters—it was a time when signals on board were given with a trumpet—bellowed forth a welcome. The Amsterdam was the first ship to be reached. The captain stood ready at the gangway to welcome the dusky sovereign, but suddenly his ship was attacked from all sides by a horde of small brown men. They swarmed over the bulwarks and hacked a dozen Hollanders to pieces before the others could defend themselves. These in turn gave fight as best they could with knives and wooden bars, but many more were killed. At last, however, the other ships managed to come to the relief of the Amsterdam, and they destroyed the fleet of war-canoes with a few volleys from their cannon. It was a sad business. Several of the officers had been killed. What with the illness of many of the men there were hardly sailors enough to man the four ships. The Amsterdam looked like a butcher shop. It was cleaned thoroughly, the dead people were given Christian burial in the open sea, and the voyage was continued to the island of Madura.

Here they arrived on the eighth of December, and were once more met by a large fleet of small craft. In one of these there was a native who knew a little Portuguese. He asked to speak to the commander, who at that moment was on the Amsterdam. Houtman told the native interpreter to row to the Mauritius, where he would join him in a few minutes. This was a good idea, for the people on the Amsterdam, who had just seen the massacre of their comrades, were very nervous and in no condition to receive another visit of natives, however friendly they intended to be. But through a mistake the boat of the interpreter did not turn toward the Mauritius, but returned once more to the Amsterdam, apparently to ask for further instructions. Then one of these horrible accidents due entirely to panic happened. The sailors of the Amsterdam opened fire upon the natives. The other ships thought that this was the sign for a new general attack, and they got out their cannon. In a moment a score of well-intentioned natives, and among them their king, had been killed or were drowning.

After this it could not be expected that the island of Madura would sell Houtman anything at all. There was only one chance left if the expedition was to be a financial success. This was a trip to the Molucca Islands. But for this voyage the ninety-four sailors who were still alive—all the others who had left Holland the year before were dead—hardly sufficed. Furthermore, the Amsterdam was beginning to show such severe leaks that the carpenters could not repair the damage. The ship was therefore beached and burned. The crew was divided among the three other ships and they set sail for the Moluccas.

Before they reached these islands a formal mutiny had broken out on board the Mauritius. Suddenly, during the afternoon meal, the captain of the ship had died. He had fainted, turned blue and black, and in less than an hour he was dead after suffering dreadful pains. Healthy people, so the sailors whispered, did not die that way, and they accused Houtman, who did not like this particular captain, of having put poison into his food. Houtman was attacked by his own men, and he was put in irons. A formal tribunal then was called together. It investigated the charges, but nothing was found against the accused Commissioner. Therefore Houtman was released, and the topsyturvy expedition once more continued its voyage.

But it never reached the Molucca Islands, for before they got to these they found the island of Bali. This proved to be governed by a well-disposed monarch. The influence of the Portuguese was less strong in this island than it had been on Java. The Hollanders, too, had learned their lesson, and they refrained from the naval swashbuckling that had often characterized their conduct on Java. On the contrary, they gave themselves every possible trouble to be very pleasant to his Majesty the Sultan. They made him fine presents, and they produced their maps of the fatherland and made a great ado about their official documents. The sultan wished to know who they were. They told him that they came from a country which was situated in the northern part of Europe, where the water turned into a solid mass across which you could drive a horse every winter. This country, according to their descriptions, covered a region occupied by Russia, France, and Germany. There was but little truth in these grandiloquent stories, but they were dealing with an innocent native who must be duly impressed by the great power and the enormous riches of the home of ninety-odd, bedraggled and much traveled Dutch sailors. The account which the sailors gave of their country so deeply impressed the king that he allowed them to buy all the spices they wanted and to collect the necessary provisions for the long return voyage. On February 26, in the second year of their voyage, the three ships got ready to sail back to Holland. One of the civilian directors who with his masterful fibbing had brought himself more particularly to the attention of his Majesty was left behind, together with one sailor. They were to act as counselors to the court, an office which they held for four years, when they returned to Amsterdam. Of the two hundred and eighty-four men who had left Holland in 1595, only eighty-nine returned after an absence of two years and four months.

That was the end of the first trip. It had not been profitable. The sale of the pepper and nutmeg bought in Bali saved the expedition from being a total loss to the investors, but there were not nearly such large revenues as were to follow in the succeeding years. Furthermore, Houtman had not been able to establish any lasting relations with any of the native princes of India. Neither could he report that the first Dutch expedition had been a shining example of tactful dealing with, or kind treatment of the people of the Indies.

But this was really a detail. It was an unfortunate incident due to their own lack of experience and to the intrigues of the rival Portuguese merchants.

From a commercial point of view this expedition was a failure. Yet it brought home a large volume of negative information which was of the utmost importance. It showed that the direct road to India was not an impossible achievement to anybody possessed of energy and courage. It showed that the power of the Portuguese in India was not as strong as had been expected. It showed that the dream of an independent colonial empire for the new Dutch Republic in the Indian islands was not an idle one. In short, it proved that all the fears and misgivings about Holland's share in the development of the riches of Asia had been unnecessary. The thing could be done.

CHAPTER V
THE SECOND VOYAGE TO INDIA—SUCCESS

There was now a great boom in the Indian trade. Whosoever could beg, borrow, or steal a few thousand guilders; whoever possessed an old scow which could perhaps be made to float, whoever was related to a man who had a cousin who had some influence on the exchange, suddenly became an Indian trader, equipped a ship, hired sailors, had mysterious conferences with nautical gentlemen who talked about their great experience in foreign waters, and then waited for the early days of spring to bid God-speed to his little expedition. Every city must have its own Indian fleet. Companies were formed, stockholders quarreled about the apportionment of the necessary capital, and at once they split up into other smaller companies. There was an "Old" Indian Trading Company. The next day there was a rival called the "New" Indian Trading Company. There was an Indian company which was backed by the province of Zeeland. There was a private enterprise of the city of Rotterdam. To be honest, there were too many companies for the small size of the country. Before another dozen years had passed they were all amalgamated into one strong commercial body, the great Dutch East India Company, but during the first years hundreds of ships stampeded to the promised land of Java and Bali and the Moluccas, and for one fleet of small vessels which came home with a profit there were a dozen which either were shipwrecked on the way or which had ruined their shareholders before they had passed the equator.

Amsterdam, as always, was the leader in this activity. It was not only a question of capital. There had to be men of vision, merchants who were willing to do things on a large scale, before such a venture could return any profit. And while the ships of the Zeeland Company were hurried to sea, and left long before the others, and incidentally came back a few years later, Amsterdam quietly collected eight hundred thousand guilders and advertised for competent officers and willing men for a large expedition. This time, it was decided, everything was to be done with scientific precision, and nothing must be left to chance. The commander in chief of the 560 men who were to take part in the expedition was Jacob van Neck, a man of good birth, excellent training, and well-known in the politics of his own city. His most important adviser was Jacob van Heemskerk, fresh from his adventures in the Arctic Sea and ready for new ones in the Indian Ocean. Several of the officers who had been to Bantam with Houtman were engaged for this second voyage. Among them our friend Van der Does, out of whose diary we copied the adventures of the first voyage to the Indies. Even the native element was not lacking. You will remember that the Hollanders had taken several hostages in Madagascar when they visited the east coast of that island in the year 1595. Two of these had been tamed and had been taken to Holland. After a year in Amsterdam they were quite willing to exchange the uncomfortable gloominess of the Dutch climate for a return to their sunny native shores. Also there was a Mohammedan boy by the name of Abdul, whom curiosity had driven from Bali to Holland on board the ship of Houtman.

The fleet of eight vessels left the roads of Texel on the first of May of the year 1598, and with a favorable wind reached the Cape Verde Islands three weeks later. There, a general council of the different captains was asked to decide upon the further course. For with each expedition the knowledge of what ought to be done and what ought to be omitted increased, and the experiences of Houtman on the coast of Africa where his entire crew had been disabled through scurvy, must not be repeated. The fleet must either follow the coast of Africa to get fresh food and water whenever necessary, or the ships must risk a more western course, which would take them a far distance away from land, but would bring them into currents which would carry them to the Indies in a shorter while. They decided to take the western course. It was a very tedious voyage except for the flying-fishes which sometimes accompanied the ship. Luck was with the expedition, and on the ninth of July the ships passed the equator. The little island of Trinidad, off the coast of Brazil, was soon reached, and an inquisitive trip in an open boat to explore this huge rock almost ended in disaster. But such small affairs as a night spent in an open boat in a stormy ocean were all in the day's work and gave the sailors something to talk about.

Within a remarkably short time the lonely island of Tristan d'Acunha was passed, and from there the current and the western winds carried the ships to the Cape of Good Hope. But near this stormy promontory a small hurricane suddenly fell upon the fleet, and after a night of very heavy squalls one of the eight ships had disappeared. It was never seen again. A few days later, this time through carelessness in observing signals, four other ships were separated from their admiral. Several days were spent in coursing about in the attempt to find them. The sea, however, is very wide, and ships very small, and Van Neck with two big and one small vessel at last decided to continue the voyage alone. He was in a hurry. There were many rivals to his great undertaking, and when he actually met a Dutch ship sent out by the province of Zeeland, he insisted that there must be no delay of any sort. The Zeeland ship, however, was not a dangerous competitor. Nine members of its crew of seventy-five had died. Among the others there was so much scurvy that only seven men were able to handle the helm. Only two could climb aloft. The Amsterdam ships ought to have helped their fellow-countrymen, but in the Indian spice trade it was a question of "first come, first served." Therefore they piously commended their Zeeland brethren to the care of the Good Lord and hastened on.

A short stay in Madagascar was necessary because the water in the tanks was of such abominable taste and smelled so badly that it must be replenished. The ships sailed to the east coast of the island, stopped at *Santa Maria*, well known from the visit of Houtman's ships three years before, and then made a short trip in search of fresh fruit to the bay of Antongil. On the island of *Santa Maria* they had found a happy population, well governed by an old king and spending their days in hunting wild animals on land or catching whales at sea. But in the Bay of Antongil things had greatly changed since Houtman had left a year before. There had been a war with some of the tribes from the interior of the island. The villages along the coast had been burned, and all the cattle had been killed. Men and women were dying of starvation. Right in the midst of the lovely tropical scenery there lay the decaying corpses of the natives, a prey to vultures and jackals. The expedition of Van Neck, however, had been sent out to buy spices in India and not to reform the heathen inhabitants of African islands. The water-tanks were hastily filled, and on the sixteenth of September the island was left to its own fate.

For two months the ships sailed eastward. There were a few sick men on board, but nobody died, which was considered a magnificent record in those days for so long a voyage. On November 19 the high mountains of the coast of Sumatra appeared upon the horizon. From there Van Neck steered southward, and near the Sunda Islands he at last reached the dangerous domains of the Portuguese. The cannon were inspected, the mechanism of the guns was well oiled, and everything was made ready for a possible fight. Before the coast of Java was reached one of the islands of the Sunda Archipelago was visited. Could the natives tell them anything about the Portuguese and their intentions? The natives could not do this, but in return asked the men whether they perhaps knew anything about a foreign expedition which had been in those parts a few years before? That expedition, it appeared, had left a very bad reputation behind on account of its cruelty and insolence.

Van Neck decided not to remain in this region, where his predecessor had made himself too thoroughly unpopular, and sailed direct for Bantam. He would take his risks. On November 26, while the sun was setting, the three ships dropped anchor in that harbor. They spent an uncomfortable night, for nobody knew what sort of reception would await them on the next day. Houtman had been in great difficulty with both the sultan and the Portuguese. Very likely the ships, flying the Dutch flag, would be attacked in the morning. But when morning came, the ubiquitous Chinaman, who in the far Indies serves foreign potentates as money-changer, merchant, diplomatic agent, and handy-man in general, came rowing out to Van

Neck's ship. He told the admiral that the sultan sent the Hollanders his very kind regards and begged them to accept a small gift of fresh fruit. The sultan was glad to see the Hollanders. If they would only send a messenger on shore the sultan would receive him at once. Meanwhile as a sign of good faith the Chinese intermediary was willing to stay on board the ship of the Hollanders. Nobody in the fleet, least of all the officers and sailors who remembered what had happened two years before, had expected such a reception. They were soon told the reason of this change in attitude. After Houtman and his ships left in the summer of 1596 the Portuguese Government had sent a strong fleet to punish the Sultan of Bantam for having been too friendly to the Hollanders. This fleet had suffered a defeat, but since that time the people in Bantam had feared the arrival of another punitive expedition. The Hollanders, therefore, came as very welcome defenders of the rights of the young sultan. It was decided that their services should be used for the defense of the harbor if the long-expected Portuguese fleet should make a new attack. It was in this rôle of the lesser of two evils that the Hollanders finally were to conquer their Indian empire from the Portuguese. Van Neck was the first Dutch captain to use the local political situation for his own benefit. He sent his representative on shore, who was received with great ceremony. He explained how this fleet had been sent to the Indies by the mighty Prince of Orange, and he promised that the Bantam government would be allowed to see all the official documents which the admiral had brought if they would deign to visit the ships. This invitation was not well received. The Bantam people had been familiar with the ways of white men for almost a hundred years. They distrusted all cordial invitations to come on board foreign ships, and they asked that the Hollanders send their papers ashore. "No," Van Neck told them through his envoy, "a document given to me by the mighty Prince of Orange is too important to be allowed out of my immediate sight."

In the end the sultan, curious to see whether these letters could perhaps tell him something of further ships which might be on their way, agreed to make his appearance upon the ship of the admiral, where he was received with great courtesy.

Then, after the fashion of the Indian ruler of his day and of our own, he demanded to know what his profits were to be in case he allowed the Hollanders to trade in his city. Van Neck began negotiations about the bribe which the different functionaries were to receive. For a consideration of 3200 reals to the sultan and the commander of the harbor, the Dutch ships were at last given permission to approach the shore and buy whatever they wanted. For ten days long canoes filled with pepper and nutmeg surrounded the ships. The pepper was bought for three reals a bag. Everything was very pleasant, but one day Abdul, the native who came from Bali, got on shore and visited the city. Here among his own people he cut quite a dash, and bragging about the wonders of the great Dutch Republic, he volunteered the information that on the Amsterdam market he had seen how a bag of pepper was sold for 100 reals. That sum, therefore, was just ninety-seven reals more than the people in Bantam received for their own raw product. Of course they did not like the idea of getting so little, and at once they refused to sell to Van Neck at the old rate. It was a great disappointment. He tried to do business with some Chinamen, but they were worse than the Javanese. They offered their pepper to the Hollanders at a ridiculously low price, but after the bags had been weighed they were found to be weighted with stones and sand and pieces of glass.

There was no end to all the small annoyances which the Dutch admiral was made to suffer. There were a number of Portuguese soldiers hanging about the town. They had been made prisoners during the last fatal expedition against Bantam, and they suffered a good many hardships. One day they were allowed to pay a visit to the Dutch ships, and the tales of their misery were so harrowing that the admiral had given them some money to be used for the purpose of buying food and clothes. No sooner, however, were the prisoners back on dry land than they started the rumor that the Hollanders were dangerous pirates and ought not to be trusted. Van Neck vowed that he would hang his ungrateful visitors if ever they came to him again with their tales of woe. Meanwhile, in order to stop further talk, he promised to raise the price of pepper two reals. For five reals a bag his ships were now filled with a cargo of the costly spice.

In a peaceful way the month of December went by. It was the last day of the year 1598 when quite unexpectedly the lost ships that had been driven away from their admiral near the Cape of

Good Hope appeared at Bantam. They had passed through many exciting adventures. After they had lost sight of the commander-in-chief, they had first spent several days trying to discover his whereabouts. Then they had continued their way to get fresh water in Madagascar. They had reached the coast of the island safely, but just before they could land a sudden storm had driven them eastward. On the seventeenth of September they had again seen land, and they had dropped their anchors to discover to what part of the world they had been blown by the wind. The map did not show that there was any land in this region. Therefore on the eighteenth of September of the year 1598 they had visited the island which lay before them, and they found that they had reached paradise. All the sailors had been taken ashore, it being Sunday, and the ships' pastor had preached a wonderful sermon. So eloquent were his words that one of the Madagascar boys who was on the fleet had accepted Christian baptism then and there. After that for a full month officers and men had taken a holiday. Whatever they wished for the island provided in abundance. There was fresh water. There were hundreds of tame pigeons. There were birds which resembled an ostrich, although they were smaller and tasted better when cooked. There were gigantic bats and turtles so large that several men could take a ride on their back. Fish abounded in the rivers and the sea around the island, and it was thickly covered with all sorts of palm-trees. Indeed, it looked so fertile that it was decided to use it as a granary for future expeditions. Grain had been planted,

and also beans and peas for the use of ships which might come during the next years. Then the island had been officially annexed for the benefit of the republic. It had been called Mauritius after Prince Maurice of Nassau, the Stadholder of Holland. Finally after a rooster and seven chickens had been given the freedom of this domain, to assure future travelers of fresh eggs, the four ships had hoisted their sails and had come to Bantam to join their admiral.

Van Neck now commanded several ships, which were loaded. But the others must await the arrival of a new supply of pepper, which was being brought to Bantam from the Moluccas by some enterprising Chinamen. This would take time, and Van Neck was still in a great hurry. He refused to consider the tempting offers of the Sultan of Bantam, who still wanted his help against his Portuguese enemies. Instead, he entered into negotiations with a Hindu merchant who offered to bring the other ships directly to the Moluccas, where they would be in the heart of the spice-growing islands. The Hindu was engaged, and navigated the ships safely to their destination. Here through their good behavior the Hollanders made such an excellent impression upon the native ruler that they were allowed to establish two settlements on shore and leave a small garrison until they should return to buy more mace and nutmeg at incredibly reasonable terms. As for Van Neck, having saluted his faithful companions with a salvo of his big guns, which started a panic in the good town of Bantam, where the people still remembered the departure of Houtman, he sailed for the coast of Africa.

He had every reason to be contented with his success. In a final audience with the governor of the city of Bantam he had promised this dignitary that the Hollanders would return the next year, "because that was the will of their mighty ruler." The governor, from his side, who upon this occasion had to deal with a much better class of men than Houtman and his crew of mutinous sailors, had decided that the Hollanders were preferable to the Portuguese, and he assured Van Neck of a cordial reception.

The return voyage was not as prosperous as the outward trip had been. Dysentery attacked the fleet, and many of the best officers and men had to be sewn into their hammocks to be dropped into the ocean, where they found an honorable burial. St. Helena, with its fresh water and its many wild animals, was reached just when the number of healthy men had fallen to thirty. A week of rest and decent food was enough to cure all the men, and then they sailed for home. But so great was the hurry of this rich squadron to reach the markets of Amsterdam that Van Neck's ship was almost destroyed when it hoisted too many sails and when the wind broke two of the masts. It was not easy to repair this damage in the open sea. After several days some sort of jury rig was equipped. The big ship, with its short stubby mast, then looked so queer that several Dutch vessels which saw it appear upon the horizon off the Gulf of Biscay beat a hasty retreat. They feared that they had to do with a new sort of pirate, sailing the seas in the most recent piratical invention.

On the nineteenth of July, after an absence of only one year and two months, the first part of Van Neck's fleet returned safely to Holland. The cargo was unloaded, and was sold on the Amsterdam exchange. After the full cost of the expedition had been paid, each of the shareholders received a profit of just one hundred per cent. Van Neck, who had established the first Dutch settlement in the Indies, was given a public reception by his good city and was marched in state to the town hall.

CHAPTER VI
VAN NOORT CIRCUMNAVIGATES THE WORLD

Oliver van Noort was the first Hollander to sail around the world. Incidentally, he was the fourth navigator to succeed in this dangerous enterprise since in the year 1520 the little ships of Magellan had accomplished the feat of circumnavigating the globe. Of the hero of this memorable Dutch voyage we know almost nothing. He was a modest man, and except for a few lines of personal introduction which appear in the printed story of his voyage, which was published in Rotterdam, his home town, in the year 1620, in which he tells us that he had made many trips to different parts of the world, his life to us is a complete mystery.

Olivier van Noort. Olivier van Noort.

He was not, like Jacob van Heemskerk and Van Neck, a man of education; neither was he of very low origin. He had picked up a good deal of learning at the common schools. Very likely he had been the mate or perhaps the captain of some small schooner, had made a little money, and then had retired from the sea. Spending one's days on board a ship in the latter half of the sixteenth century was no pleasure. The ships were small. The cabins were uncomfortable, and so low that nowhere one could stand up straight. Cooking had to be done on a very primitive stove, which could not always be used when the weather was bad. The middle part of the deck was apt to be flooded most of the time, and the flat-bottomed ships rolled and pitched horribly. Therefore, as soon as a man had made a little competency as the master of a small craft he was apt to look for some quiet occupation on shore. He had not learned a regular trade which he could use on shore. Very often, therefore, he opened a small hotel or an inn or just an ale-house where he could tell yarns about whales and wild men and queer countries which he had seen in the course of his peregrinations. And when the evening came and the tired citizen wanted to smoke a comfortable pipe and discuss the politics of the pope, the emperor, kings, dukes, bishops and their Mightinesses, his own aldermen, he liked to do so under the guidance of a man who knew what was what in the world and who could compare the stadholder's victories over the Spaniards with those which King Wunga Wunga of Mozambique had gained over his Hottentot neighbors, and who knew that the wine of Oporto sold in Havana for less than the vinegar from Dantsic and the salted fish from Archangel.

Therefore we are not surprised when in the year 1595 we find Oliver van Noort described as the owner of the "Double White Keys," an ale-house in the town of Rotterdam. He might have finished his days there in peace and prosperity, but when Houtman returned from his first voyage and the craze for the riches of the Indies, or at least a share thereof, struck the town of Rotterdam, Van Noort, together with everybody else who could borrow a few pennies, began to think of new ways of reaching the marvelous island of Java, made of gold and jewels and the even more valuable pepper and nutmeg. Van Noort himself possessed some money and the rest he obtained from several of his best customers. With this small sum he founded a trading company of his own. He petitioned the estates general of the republic and the estates of his own province of Holland to assist him in an expedition toward the "Kingdom of Chili, the west coast of America, and if need be, the islands of the Moluccas." To make this important enterprise successful, the estates general were asked to give Van Noort and his trading company freedom of export and import for at least six voyages, and to present it with ten cannon and twelve thousand pounds of gunpowder. He asked for much in the hope of obtaining at least part of what he desired.

In the winter of 1597 his request was granted. He received four guns, six thousand pounds of bullets, twelve thousand pounds of gunpowder, and a special grant which relieved him of the customary export tax for two voyages. This demand for cannon, gunpowder, and bullets gives us the impression that the expedition expected to meet with serious trouble. That was quite true. The southern part of America was the private property of the Spaniards and the Portuguese. Anybody who ventured into those regions flying the Dutch colors did so at his own peril. Among his fellow-citizens Van Noort had the reputation of great courage. Nobody knew any precise details of his early life, but it was whispered, although never proved, that many years ago, long before the days of Houtman, he had tried to reach the Indies all alone, but that he had preferred the more lucrative profession of pirate to the dangerous calling of the pioneer. Since, however, all his privateering had been done at the expense of the Spaniards, nobody minded these few alleged irregularities of his youthful days. And the merchants who drank their pot of ale at his inn willingly provided him with the money which he needed, bade him go ahead, and helped him when during the winter of the year 1597 he was getting his two ships ready for the voyage.

Now, it happened that at that time a number of merchants in Amsterdam were working for the same purpose. They, too, wanted to sail to the Moluccas by way of the Strait of Magellan. For the sake of greater safety the two companies decided to travel together. In June of the year 1597 their fleet, composed of four ships, was ready for the voyage. Van Noort was to command the biggest vessel, the Mauritius, while the commander of the Amsterdam company was to be vice-admiral of the fleet on board the Henrick Frederick. The name of the vice-admiral was Jacob Claesz. We know nothing about his early career, but we know all the details of his tragic end. There were two other small ships. There was a yacht called the Eendracht, and there was a merchantman called the Hope. The tonnage of the ships is not mentioned, but since there were only two hundred and forty-eight men on the four ships, they must have been small even for that time.

In a general way our meager information about the invested capital, the strange stories of the early lives of the commanders, and the very rough character of the crew show that we have to do with one of the many mushroom companies, an enterprise which was not based upon very sound principles, but was of a purely speculative nature. During the earliest days of Indian trading, however, all good merchants were in such a hurry to make money to get to Java long before anybody else and to reach home ahead of all competitors that there was no time for the promoting of absolutely sound companies.

On the other hand, the men who commanded those first expeditions had all been schooled in the noble art of self-reliance during the first twenty terrible years of the war against Spain. They were brave, they were resourceful, they succeeded where others, more careful, would have failed.

On the twenty-eighth of June of the year 1597 Van Noort left Rotterdam to await his companions from Amsterdam in the Downs, England. He waited for several weeks, but the ships did not appear, so he went back to Holland to find out what might have become of them. He found them lying at anchor in one of the Zeeland streams. Evidently there had been a misunderstanding as to the exact meeting-place of the two squadrons. Together they then began the voyage for a second time. They had lost a month and a half in waiting for each other, but at that date forty-five days more or less did not matter. The trip was to take a couple of years, anyway.

First of all Van Noort went to Plymouth, where he had arranged to meet a British sailor, commonly referred to as "Captain Melis," a

man who had been around the world with Captain Cavendish in 1588, and who was familiar with the stormy regions around the southern part of the American continent. In exchange for one Englishman, Van Noort lost several good Dutchmen. Six of his sailors deserted, and could not be found again.

The first part of the trip was along the coast of Africa, a road which we know from other expeditions. Then came a story with which we are only too familiar from previous accounts, for the much dreaded scurvy appeared among the men. When the fleet passed the small island of Principe in the Gulf of Guinea, it was decided to land there and try to obtain fresh water and fresh food. Unfortunately, this island was within the established domain of the Portuguese, and the Hollanders must be careful. Early in the morning of the day on which they intended to look for water they sent three boats ashore flying a white flag as a sign of their peaceful intentions. The inhabitants of the island came near the boats, also carrying a white flag. They informed the Hollanders that if they would kindly visit the near-by villages the natives would sell them everything they wanted, provided the Hollanders paid cash. The men were ordered to stay near the boats, but four officers went farther inland. They were asked to come first of all to the Portuguese castle that was on the island. They went, but once inside, they were suddenly attacked, and three of them were murdered. The fourth one jumped out of the gate just in time to save his life. He ran to the shore. This was a great loss to the Hollanders, for among the men who had been killed was a brother of Admiral van Noort and the English pilot upon whom they depended to guide them through the difficult Strait of Magellan.

To uphold the prestige of the Dutch Republic, Van Noort decided to make an example. The next day after he landed with 120 of his men and entrenched himself near the mouth of a river, so that he might fill his water-tanks at leisure. Then, following this river, he went into the interior of the country and burned down all the plantations and houses he could find.

Well provided with fresh water, he thereupon crossed the Atlantic Ocean and steered for the coast of Brazil. On the ninth of February he dropped anchor in the harbor of Rio de Janeiro, which was a Portuguese town. He carefully kept out of reach of the menacing guns of the fortification. The reception in Brazil was little more cordial than it had been on the other side of the ocean. The Portuguese sent a boat to the Dutch ships to ask what they wanted. The answer was that the Hollanders were peaceful travelers in need of fresh provisions. The provisions were promised for the next day, but Van Noort, who had heard similar promises before, was on his guard and for safety's sake he kept a few Portuguese sailors on his ship as hostages.

On the morning of the next day he sent several of his men to the shore to get the supplies. They landed near a mountain called the Sugarloaf. Once more the Portuguese did not play the game fairly. They had posted a number of their soldiers in a well-hidden ambush near the Sugarloaf. These soldiers suddenly opened fire, wounded a large number of the Dutch seamen and took two of them prisoners. A little later a shot fired from one of the cannon of the castle killed a man on board the Eendracht. The two Dutch prisoners were safely returned the next day in exchange for the Portuguese hostages, but Van Noort was obliged to leave the town without getting his provisions. Therefore a few days later he landed on a small island near the coast where he found water and fruit, and his men caught fish and wild birds and were happy. Again the Portuguese interfered. They had ordered a number of Indians to follow the Dutch fleet and do whatever damage they could. When a Dutch boat with six men came rowing to the shore it was suddenly attacked by a large number of Indians in canoes. Two of the six men were killed. The other four were taken prisoner and were never seen again.

Of course adventures of this sort were not very encouraging. Some of the officers suggested that, after all, it might be a better idea to discontinue the voyage around the South American coast before it was too late. They proposed that the ships should cross the Atlantic once more, and should either go to St. Helena and wait there until the next spring or should sail to India by way of the Cape of Good Hope; for it was now the month of March, and in that part of the world our summer is winter and our winter is summer. Wherefore they greatly feared that the ships could not reach the Strait of Magellan before the winter storms of July should set in. It was upon such occasions that Van Noort showed his courage and his resolute spirit. His expedition was in bad shape. One of the ships, the Eendracht, was leaking badly. Through the bad water, the hard work, and the

insufficient food a large number of sailors had fallen ill, and every day some of them died. Wherever the expedition tried to land on the coast of Brazil to get water and supplies they found strong Portuguese detachments which drove them away. Not for a moment, however, did Van Noort dream of giving up his original plans.

At last, after many weeks and by mere chance, he found a little island called St. Clara where there were no Portuguese and no unfriendly natives and where he could build a fort on shore to land the sick men and cure them of their scurvy with fresh herbs. The expedition remained on Santa Clara for three weeks. Gradually the strength of the men returned, but they were still very weak, and it was now necessary that they should get plenty of exercise in the open air. Therefore the admiral ordered the kitchens to be built at a short distance from the fort. Those men who walked out to the kitchen got more dinner than those who demanded that their food be brought to them. Soon they all walked, and they greatly benefited by this little scheme of their commander. On June 28 they were able to go back to the ship, and then they set sail for the south. Two men, however, who had caused trouble since the beginning of the voyage and who seemed to be incorrigible were left behind on the island to get home as best they could. They never did. Even such a severe punishment was not a deterrent. A few days later a sailor attacked and wounded one of the officers with a knife. He was spiked to the mast with the same knife stuck through his right hand. Then he was left standing until he had pulled the knife out himself. It was a very rough crew, and only a system of discipline enforced in this cruel fashion saved the officers from being murdered and thrown overboard, so that the men might return home or become pirates.

I have just mentioned the bad condition of the Eendracht. The ship was so unseaworthy, and so great was the danger of drowning all on board, that Van Noort at last decided to sacrifice the vessel. The sailors were divided among the other ships, and the Eendracht was burned off the coast of Brazil.

Van Noort now reached the southern part of the American continent.

The Strait of Magellan had been discovered in 1530. But even in the year 1598 it was little known. The few mariners who had passed through had all told of the difficulty of navigating these narrows, with their swift currents running from ocean to ocean and their terrible storms, not to speak of the fog. Crossing from the Atlantic into the Pacific was therefore something which was considered a very difficult feat, and Van Noort did not dare to risk it with his ships in their bad condition. He made for the little Island of Porto Deseado, which Cavendish had discovered only a few years before. There was a sand-bank near the coast, and upon this the ships were anchored at high tide. Then, when the tide fell, the ships were left on the dry sand, and the men had several hours in which to clean, tar, and calk them and generally overhaul everything that needed repairing. On the shore of the island a regular smithy was constructed. For three months everybody worked hard to get the vessels in proper condition for the dangerous voyage.

While they were on the island the captain of the Hope died. He was buried with great solemnity, and the former captain of the Eendracht was made commander of the Hope, which was rebaptized the Eendracht. This word means harmony in Dutch, and the Good Lord knows that they needed harmony during the many difficult months which were to follow. On November 5, fourteen months after Van

Noort left Holland, and when the number of his men had been reduced to 148, he at last reached the Strait of Magellan. The ship of the admiral entered the strait first, and was followed by the new Eendracht. The Henrick Frederick, however, commanded by Jacob Claesz, the vice-admiral, went her own way. Van Noort signaled to this ship to keep close to the Mauritius, but he never received an answer. Van Noort then ordered Claesz to come to the admiral's vessel and give an account of himself. The only answer which he received to that message was that Captain Claesz was just as good as Admiral van Noort, and was going to do just exactly what he pleased.

This was a case of open rebellion, but Van Noort was so busy navigating the difficult current that he could not stop to make an investigation. Four times his ship was driven back by the strong wind. At the fifth attempt the ship at last passed the first narrows and anchored well inside the strait. The next day they passed a high mountain which they called Cape Nassau, and where they saw many natives running toward the shore. The natives in the southern part of the continent were not like the ordinary Indian with whom the Hollanders were familiar. They were very strong and brave and caused the Hollanders much difficulty. They handled bows and arrows well, and their coats, made of skin, gave them a general appearance of greater civilization than anybody had expected to find in this distant part of the world. When the Dutch sailors rowed to the shore of the strait, the Indians attacked them at once. It was an unequal battle of arrows against bullets. The natives were driven back into their mountains, where they defended themselves in front of a large hollow rock. At last, however, all the men had been killed, and then the sailors discovered that the grotto was filled with many women and children. They did not harm these, but captured four small boys and two little girls to take home to Holland. It seems to have been an inveterate habit of early expeditions to distant countries to take home some natives as curiosities. Beginning with Columbus, every explorer had brought a couple of natives with him when he returned home. The poor things usually died of small-pox or consumption or some other civilized disease. In case they kept alive, they became a sort of nondescript town-curiosity. What Van Noort intended to do with little Patagonians in Rotterdam I do not know, but he had half a dozen on board when on November 28 his two ships reached the spot where they expected to find a strong Spanish castle.

This fortress, so they knew, had been built after the attack of Drake on the west coast of America. Drake's expedition had caused a panic among the Spanish settlements of Chile and Peru. Orders had come from Madrid to fortify the Strait of Magellan and close the narrows to all foreign vessels. A castle had been built and a garrison had been sent. Then, however, as happened often in Spain, the home government had forgotten all about this isolated spot. No provisions had been forwarded. The country itself, being barren and cold, did not raise anything which a Spaniard could eat. After a few years the castle had been deserted. When Cavendish sailed through the strait he had taken the few remaining cannon out of the ruins. Van Noort did not even find the ruins. Two whole months Van Noort spent in the strait. He took his time in this part of the voyage. He dropped anchor in a bay which he called Olivier's Bay, and there began to build some new life-boats.

After a few days the mutinous Henrick Frederick also appeared in this bay. Van Noort asked Claesz to come on board his ship and explain his strange conduct. The vice-admiral refused to obey. He was taken prisoner, and brought before a court-martial. We do not know the real grounds for the strange conduct of Claesz. He might have known that discipline in those days meant something brutally severe; and yet he disobeyed his admiral's positive orders, and when he was brought before the court-martial he could not or would not defend himself. He was found guilty, and he was condemned to be put on shore. He was given some bread and some wine, and when the fleet sailed away he was left behind all alone. There was of course a chance that another ship would pick him up. A few weeks before other Dutch ships had been in the strait. But this chance was a very small one, and the sailors of Van Noort knew it. They said a prayer for the soul of their former captain who was condemned to die a miserable death far away from home. Yet no one objected to this punishment. Navigation to the Indies in the sixteenth century was as dangerous as war, and insubordination could not be tolerated, not even when the man who refused to obey orders was one of the original investors of the expedition and second in command.

On the twenty-ninth of February Van Noort reached the Pacific. The last mile from the strait into the open sea took him four weeks. He now sailed northward along the coast of South America. Two weeks later, during a storm, the Henrick Frederick disappeared. Such an occurrence had been foreseen. Van Noort had told his captains to meet him near the island of *Santa Maria* in case they should become separated from him during the night or in a fog. Therefore he did not worry about the fate of the ship, but sailed for the coast of Chile.

After a short visit and a meeting with some natives, who told him that they hated the Spaniards and welcomed the Hollanders as their defenders against the Spanish oppressors, Van Noort reached the island of *Santa Maria*. In the distance he saw a ship. Of course he thought that this must be his own lost vessel waiting for him; but when he came near, the strange ship hoisted her sails and fled. It was a Spaniard called the Buen Jesus. The Dutch admiral could not allow this ship to escape. It might have warned the Spanish admiral in Lima, and then Van Noort would have been obliged to fight the entire Spanish Pacific fleet. The Eendracht was ordered to catch the Buen Jesus. This she did, for the Dutch ships could sail faster than the Spanish ones, though they were smaller. Van Noort had done wisely. The Spaniard was one of a large fleet detailed to watch the arrival of the Dutch vessels. The year before another Dutch fleet had reached the Pacific. It suffered a defeat at the hands of the Spaniards. This had served as a warning. The Hollanders did not have the reputation of giving up an enterprise when once they had started upon it, and the Spanish fleet was kept cruising in the southern part of the Pacific to destroy whatever Dutch ships might try to enter the private domains of Spain.

From that moment Van Noort's voyage and his ships in the Pacific were as safe as a man smoking a pipe in a powder-magazine. They might be destroyed at any moment. As a best means of defense, the Hollanders decided to make a great show of strength. They did not wait for the assistance of the Henrick Frederick, but sailed at once to Valparaiso, took several Spanish ships anchored in the roads, and burned all of the others except one, which was added to the Dutch fleet. From the captain of the Buen Jesus Van Noort had heard that a number of Hollanders were imprisoned in the castle of Valparaiso. He sent ashore, asking for information, and he received letters from a Dutchman, asking for help.

Van Noort, however, was too weak to attack the town, but he thought that something might be done in this case through kindness. So he set all the crew of the Buen Jesus except the mate free, and him he kept as an hostage, and sent the men to the Spanish commander with his compliments. Thereupon he continued his voyage, but was careful to stay away from Lima, where he knew there were three large Spanish vessels waiting for him. Instead of that, he made for the Cape of San Francisco, where he hoped to capture the Peruvian silver fleet. Quite accidentally, however, he discovered that he was about to run into another trap. Some Negro slaves who had been on board the Buen Jesus, and who were now with Van Noort, spread the rumor that more than fifty thousand pounds of gold which had been on the Buen Jesus had been thrown overboard just before the Hollanders captured the vessel. The mate of the ship was still on the Mauritius, and he was asked if this was true. He denied it, but he denied it in such a fashion that it was hard to believe him. Therefore he was tortured. Not very much, but just enough to make him desirous of telling the truth. He then told that the gold had actually been on board the Buen Jesus; and since he was once confessing, he volunteered further information, and now told Van Noort that the captain of the Buen Jesus and he had arranged to warn the Spanish fleet to await the Hollanders near Cape San Francisco and to attack them there while the Hollanders were watching the coast of Peru for the Peruvian silver fleet. No further information was wanted, and the Spaniard was released. He might have taken this episode as a warning to be on his good behavior. Thus far he had been well treated. He slept and took his meals in Van Noort's own cabin. But soon afterward he tried to start a mutiny among the Negro slaves who had served with him on the Spanish man-of-war. Without further trial he was then thrown overboard.

The expedition against the silver fleet, however, had to be given up. It would have been too dangerous. It became necessary to leave the eastern part of the Pacific and to cross to the Indies as fast as possible. The Spanish ship which had been captured in Valparaiso proved to be a bad sailor and was burned. The two Dutch ships, with a crew of about a hundred men, sailed alone for the Marianne Islands. Some travelers have called these islands the Ladrones. That means the islands of the Thieves, and the natives who came flocking out to the ships showed that they deserved this designation. They were very nimble-fingered, and they stole whatever they could find. They would climb on board the ships of Van Noort, take some knives or merely a piece of old iron, and before anybody could prevent them they had dived overboard and had disappeared under water. All day long their little canoes swarmed around the Dutch ships. They offered many things for sale, but they were very dishonest in trade, and the rice they sold was full of stones, and the bottoms of their rice baskets were filled with cocoanuts. Two days were spent getting fresh water and buying food, and then Van Noort sailed for the Philippine Islands. On the fourteenth of October of the year 1600 he landed on the eastern coast of Luzon.

By this time the Dutch ships were in the heart of the Spanish colonies, and it was necessary to be very careful not to be detected as Hollanders. The natives on shore, who had seen them in the distance, warned the Spanish authorities, and early in the morning a sloop rowed by natives brought a Spanish officer.

Van Noort arranged a fine little comedy for his benefit. He hoisted the Spanish flag and he dressed a number of his men in cowls, so that they would look like monks. These peeped over the bulwarks when the Spaniard came near, mumbling their prayers with great devotion.

Van Noort himself, with the courtesy of the professional innkeeper, received his guest, and in fluent French told him that his ship was French and that he was trading in this part of the Indies with the special permission of his Majesty the Spanish king. He regretted to inform his visitor that his first mate had just died and that he did not know exactly in which part of the Indies his ship had landed. Furthermore he told the Spaniard that he was sadly in need of provisions and this excellent boarding officer was completely taken in by the comedy and at once gave Van Noort rice and a number of live pigs. The next day a higher officer made his appearance. Again that story of being a French ship was told, and, what is more, was believed. Van Noort was allowed to buy what he wanted and to drop anchor on the coast. To expedite his work, he sent one of his sailors who spoke Spanish fluently to the shore. This man reported that the Spaniards never even considered the possibility of an attack by Dutch ships so far away from home and so well protected by their fleet in the Pacific. Everything seemed safe.

But at last the Spaniards, who had heard a lot about the wonderful commission given to this strange captain by the King of France and the King of Spain, but who had never seen it, became curious. Quite suddenly they sent a captain accompanied by a learned priest who could verify the documents. It was a difficult case for the Dutch admiral. His official letters were all signed by the man with whom Spain was in open warfare, Prince Maurice of Nassau. When this name was found at the bottom of Van Noort's documents, his little comedy was over. Nobody thereafter was allowed to leave the ship, and the natives were forbidden to trade with the Hollander. Van Noort, however, had obtained the supplies he needed. He had an abundance of fresh provisions, and two natives had been hired to act as pilot in the straits between the different Philippine Islands.

The next few weeks Van Noort actually spent among those islands, and with his two ships terribly battered after a voyage of more than two years of travel he spread terror among the Spaniards. Many ships were taken, and landing parties destroyed villages and houses. Finally he even dared to sail into the Bay of Manila. Under the guns of the Spanish fleet he set fire to a number of native ships, and then spent several days in front of the harbor taking the cargo out of the ships which came to the Spanish capital to pay tribute. As a last insult, he sent a message to the Spanish governor to tell him that he intended to visit his capital shortly, and then got ready to depart for further conquest. He had waited just a few hours too long and he had been just a trifle too brave, for before he could get ready for battle his ships were attacked by two large Spanish men-of-war. The Mauritius was captured. That is to say, the Spaniards drove all the Hollanders from her deck and jumped on board. But the crew fought so bravely from below with guns and spears and small cannon that the Spaniards were driven back to their own ship. It was a desperate fight. If the Hollanders had been taken prisoner, they would have been hanged without trial. Van Noort encouraged his men, and told them that he would blow up the ship before he would surrender. Even those who were wounded fought like angry cats. At last a lucky shot from the Mauritius hit the largest Spaniard beneath the water-line. It was the ship of the admiral of Manila, and at once began to sink. There was no hope for any one on board her. In the distance Van Noort could see that the Eendracht, which had only twenty-five men, had just been taken by the other Spanish ship. With his own wounded crew he could not go to her assistance. To save his own vessel, he was obliged to escape as fast as possible. He hoisted his sails as well as he could with the few sailors who had been left unharmed. Of fifty-odd men five were dead and twenty-six were badly wounded. Right through the quiet sea, strewn with pieces of wreckage and scores of men clinging to masts and boxes and tables, the Mauritius made her way. With cannon and guns and spears the survivors on the Mauritius killed as many Spaniards as possible. The others were left to drown. Then the ship was cleaned, the dead Spaniards were thrown overboard, and piloted by two Chinese traders who were picked up during the voyage, Van Noort safely reached the coast of Borneo. Here the natives almost succeeded in killing the rest of his men. In the middle of the night they tried to cut the cables of the last remaining anchor. The Mauritius would have been driven on shore, and the natives could have plundered her at leisure; but their plan was discovered by the Hollanders. A second attempt to hide eighty well-armed men in a large canoe which was pretending to bring a gift of several oxen came to nothing when the natives saw that Van Noort's men made ready to fire their cannon.

La bataille La bataille d'dutre nous et contpe sieux de Manille faicte le 14 Decembre ano 1600

Another year had now gone by. It was January of 1601, and Van Noort's condition was still very dangerous. There were no supplies on board. The Chinese pilots did not know the coast of Borneo. There were many islands and many straits, and Van Noort had lost all idea

as to his exact position. When he met a Chinese vessel on the way to India he forced it to heave to and stole the mate, who was an experienced sailor. Then the wind suddenly refused to blow from the right direction, and it was many weeks before the Mauritius reached the harbor of Cheribon, in the central part of Java, many miles away from Bantam.

Van Noort called upon his few remaining officers to decide what they ought to do. If his expedition were to be a financial success, he must find some place where he could buy spices. Bantam was near by, but according to the stories of Houtman and his expedition, the people in Bantam were very unfriendly. With his twenty-three men the Dutch commander did not dare to risk another battle. It is true that since the visit of Houtman his successor Van Neck had established very good relations with the sultan; but Van Noort had been away from home for over three years, and knew nothing of Van Neck's voyage.

He might have guessed that there were Hollanders in Bantam when he found that there were no spices to be had in any of the other Javanese ports. Wherever he went he heard the same story. All the spices were now being sent to Bantam, where the Hollanders paid a very high price for them. But Van Noort distrusted this report. It might be another plot of the Portuguese to catch him, and to keep out of harm's way, he sailed through the straits of Bali, avoided the north coast of Java and went to the Cape of Good Hope.

The home trip was the most successful part of the entire voyage. It is true that, without good instruments, the Dutch ships once more lost their bearings. They thought that they were two hundred miles away from the coast of Africa when they had already passed the cape. On the twenty-sixth of May Van Noort landed at St. Helena. Three weeks later he met a large fleet. The ships flew the Dutch flag. They were part of a squadron commanded by Jacob van Heemskerk, outward bound for their second voyage to India. From them the Hollanders got their first news from home; how Van Neck's expedition had been a great success,

and how Bantam, which had been carefully avoided, was now a Dutch settlement. Van Noort told them of his fight with the Spanish fleet in different parts of the Pacific, and in turn he was informed of the great victory which Prince Maurice had just won over the Spaniards near Nieuwpoort which had assured the Dutch Republic its final liberty. Then both fleets continued their voyage. On the twenty-eighth of August Van Noort and forty-four out of the two hundred and forty-eight who had sailed away with him three years before came back to Rotterdam.

Cite de Borneo La baye de Isle et Cite de Borneo. Bapt. a Deutechum fec.

The next year a few other men who had belonged to the expedition reached Holland. They had served on the Henrick Frederick which had disappeared just after Van Noort had left the Strait of Magellan. They had waited for their commander near the island of *Santa Maria*, but the arrival of the Spanish man-of-war had spoiled all idea of meeting each other on that spot. The Henrick Frederick had crossed the Pacific alone. Many of her men had died, and the others were so weak that when they reached the Moluccas they could no longer handle the ship. They had sold it to the Sultan of Ternate for some bags of nutmeg, and with a small sloop of their own construction they had reached Bantam in April of the year 1602. There they had found a part of the same fleet of Heemskerk which Van Noort had met on the coast of Africa. On one of the ships many sailors had just died. Their place had been offered to the men of the old Henrick Frederick. In the winter of 1602 they returned to their home city.

That ended one of the most famous of the expeditions which tried to establish for the Hollanders a new route to the Indies through the Strait of Magellan. But while Van Noort was in the Pacific the route of the cape had proved to be such a great and easy success that further attempts to reach Java and the Moluccas by way of the Strait of Magellan were hereafter given up. The Pacific trading companies were changed into ordinary Indian companies which sent all their ships around the cape. As for Van Noort, who was the first Hollander to sail around the world, he entered the naval service of the republic, and had a chance to practise his very marked ability as a leader of men in more dangerous circumstances. As an Indian trader he would not have been a great success. The old irresponsible buccaneering days of that trade were gone forever. The difficult art of founding a commercial empire by persuasion rather than by force was put into the hands of men who were not only brave, but also tactful.

CHAPTER VII
THE ATTACK UPON THE WEST COAST OF AMERICA

This is the story of another expedition which tried to get possession of the Indian route by way of the Strait of Magellan. It was a sad business.

Oliver Van Noort, although he met with many difficulties, managed to bring one ship home and added greatly to the fame of the Dutch navigators. But the second expedition, equipped by two of the richest men of Rotterdam and sent out under the best of auspices, proved to be a total failure. The capital of half a million guilders which had been invested was an absolute loss. Most of the participants in the voyage died. The ships were lost. Perhaps everything had been prepared just a trifle too carefully. Van Noort, with his little ships, knew that he had to depend upon his own energy and resourcefulness; but the captains of the five ships which left Rotterdam on the twenty-seventh of July, 1598, with almost five hundred men were under the impression that half of the work had been done at home by the owners. Perhaps, too, there is such a thing as luck in navigating the high seas. One fleet sails for the Indies and has good weather all the way across the ocean. When the wind blows hard it blows from the right direction. The next squadron which leaves two weeks later meets with storms and suffers from one unfortunate accident after the other; everybody gets sick, and when the sailors look for relief on land they find nothing but a barren desert. And so it goes. It is not for us to complain, but to recite faithfully the sad adventures of the good ships the Hoop, the Liefde, the Geloof, the Trouwe, and the Blyde Boodschap, all of which tried very hard to accomplish what Van Noort had been allowed to do with much less trouble.

The ships, as we said, left Rotterdam in July, and after two months they reached the Cape Verde Islands. There they found a couple of ships from Hamburg, for the Germans at the early period of exploring and discoveries were very active sailors. A few years later, however, the Thirty Years' War was to destroy their seafaring enterprises for centuries at least.

Near these islands the Hollanders had their first encounter with the Portuguese. The stories of such meetings between the early Dutch navigators and the Portuguese owners of African and Asiatic islands always read the same way. The Hollanders ask for leave to go on shore to get fresh water and to buy provisions. This leave is never granted. Then the two parties fight each other. In most cases the Hollanders are victorious, though they still have too much respect for the traditional power of the Portuguese to risk a definite attack upon their strongholds. Very slowly and only after many years of experiment do they venture to drive the Portuguese out of their colonies and take possession of this large, but badly managed, empire.

When our five Dutch ships reached the island of San Thome they sent a messenger to the Portuguese commander and asked him, please, to give them some fresh water. The Portuguese told the Hollanders to wait. But they could not wait, for the water on board the ships had all been used up. Therefore they landed with one hundred and fifty men and charged the hill upon which the Portuguese had built a fortress. The garrison was forced to surrender. Before any more fighting took place the Portuguese offered to treat the Hollanders as welcome guests if they would sail to the next harbor of San Iago, where there was an abundance of stores and where general provisions were for sale at reasonable prices. This proposal was accepted. The sailors went back to their ships and made for San Iago. The wind, however, was not favorable, and they did not reach their destination until the hour appointed to meet the Portuguese officials had passed. When they arrived near the shore they noticed that the soldiers on land were very active and had placed a number of cannon in an ambush from which they could destroy the Dutch ships as soon as they should have dropped anchor. This, of course, was a breach of good faith. So back they went to their first landing-place. They landed, filled all their water-tanks, took the corn stored in a small storehouse, killed several Portuguese, caught a large number of turtles for the sick people on board, and hoisted sail to cross the Atlantic Ocean.

And then the bad luck which was to follow this expedition began. The admiral of the fleet, Jacques Mahu, died suddenly of a fever and was buried at sea. Two weeks later so many men were desperately ill with the same fever that the ships were obliged to return upon their own track and establish a hospital upon one of the islands off the coast of Guinea. All this time the wind blew from the wrong direction. When at last they saw land, they found that they were near the coast of Lower Guinea. They sent a boat to the shore to discover some native tribe which owned cattle. But the natives, who feared all white men as possible slave-dealers, ran into the bushes and carefully took their possessions with them. Fortunately, after a few days another Dutch ship appeared upon the horizon, and the first mate of this vessel, a Frenchman by birth, knew the language of the negroes. Through him a message was sent to the king of a small tribe, and when it had been proved that the Hollanders were not slave-dealers, but honest merchants on their way to the Indies and willing to pay money for whatever they bought, their newly elected commander, Sebalt de Weert was received in state and invited to dine with his Majesty.

This dinner, much to the regret of the hungry guests, was a poor affair. The negro chieftain tried to be very civil to his guests. In their honor he had powdered himself white with the ashes of a wood fire, but the food was neither abundant nor very good. The Hollanders decided to invite his Majesty to one of their own dinners as a good example and a hint. From among the few supplies which were left on board they arranged so excellent a dinner that his royal Highness ate everything on the table and then fell fast asleep in his chair. But when the next day the Hollanders tried to buy the fresh provisions which they expected to get, they found that the domains of the king produced nothing but one single goat, a lean goat at that, and four puny chickens.

The coast of Guinea, sometimes called the "dry Gallows," gets its agreeable reputation from the fact that the malarial fevers of this swampy region usually kill all the white people who venture to settle there. The new commander of the expedition caught this malaria, and was sick in his bed for over two months. Sixteen of his sailors died, and finally the expedition was obliged to flee to the healthy islands, which of course belonged to the Portuguese. Early in December they sailed toward Annabon. Once again the Portuguese refused them both water and food. A troop of men were landed to take by force what they could not obtain through an appeal to Christian charity. The Portuguese did not await this attack, but surrendered their fortress and fled toward the mountains. From there they arranged sniping expeditions which killed many Hollanders. As a punishment, Admiral de Weert burned the white settlement and the church. He took all the provisions which were stored in the little town, and on the second of January of the year 1599 he tried once more to cross the Atlantic Ocean.

This time the wind was favorable. Soon the ships had passed out of the hot equatorial regions. The sailors who had suffered from scurvy and malaria began to feel better in the colder climate of the Argentinian coast. They recovered so fast and they had such a great appetite after their long-enforced fast that many of them threatened to die from over-feeding. And one poor fellow who was so hungry that he stole bread at night from the ship's pantry was publicly hanged to stop further theft of the meager supplies. When the ships were near the coast of South America things went wrong once more. First of all the sailors were frightened by the sudden appearance of what they supposed to be blood upon the surface of the ocean. As far as the eye could reach, the water was of a dark-red color. This phenomenon, however, proved to be caused by billions of little plants. They made the water look quite horrible, but they were entirely harmless. A few days later one of the men, an Englishman, while at dinner suddenly uttered a dreadful scream and fell backward, dead. The next day another one of the sailors suddenly became insane and tried to scratch and bite everybody who came near him. After three days his condition improved somewhat, but he never recovered his reason. When he was put to bed at night he would not allow himself to be covered up. One very cold night both his feet were frozen and had to be amputated. That was the end of the poor fellow. He did not survive the operation.

It was a sad expedition which at last reached the Strait of Magellan on the sixth of April of the year 1599. Happily the weather near the strait was fine. There was plenty of fresh water on the shore. The men killed hundreds of birds, caught geese and ducks, and found a large supply of oysters. But when finally the day came on which they tried to enter the strait, the wind suddenly veered around, and during four months the ships were forced to stay in their little harbor. They had enough to eat and they had found wood to keep warm, but much valuable time was lost, and when the winter at last came upon them with sudden violence they were entirely unprepared for it. The reports of the expeditions of Magellan and Drake and Cavendish had shown that an expedition around the world was apt to suffer from too much heat, but rarely from too much cold. Except for the few miles of the Strait of Magellan, the ships sailed in tropical or semi-tropical regions all the time. Therefore the Dutch ships had not brought any heavy clothes or furs, which would have taken up a lot of room, and the food which had been put up for them in Holland had been prepared with the idea of supporting men who did their work under a blazing sun. When they were obliged to live for a long time in a raw, cold climate and work hard, hunting and fishing and gathering wood amid snow and icy winds, the sailors did not get sufficient nourishment. From sheer misery and exposure one hundred and twenty men died within less than four months. Among them was the captain of the Trouwe. He was the second officer to perish before his ship had reached the Pacific Ocean.

But illness was not the only enemy of this expedition. The natives of the south coast joined the terrible climate in its attack upon the Hollanders. They murdered Dutch sailors when these had gone on shore to look for fire-wood or to examine their traps. They killed several men and they wounded more. Being wounded was almost as bad as being killed outright, for the spears of the natives were made with nasty barbs which caused very bad wounds. When they once had penetrated into a man's arm or hand, the only way to get them out successfully was by pushing them through until they came out again at the other side, or cut away all the flesh, in both cases a very painful operation.

At last, on the twentieth of August, the wind turned, and the ships were able to enter the strait. The joy of the men did not last very long. The next day there was no wind at all, and once more the fleet anchored. To keep his few remaining men busy, the commander arranged an expedition on shore. It was the first time that a Dutch fleet had been in this part of the world, and the event must be properly celebrated. A high pole was planted in a conspicuous spot on shore, and the adventures of the expedition and the names of the leaders were carved on the pole. Near this pole a small cemetery was made where two sailors who had died the night before were buried. In the evening all went back to their ships. When they returned the next morning, they found that the natives had hacked the monument to pieces and the corpses of the dead Hollanders had been dug out of the earth and had been cut into little bits and were spread all over the shore. This humiliating experience was the last one which they suffered in the strait. The wind at last turned to their advantage and on the third of September the ships reached the Pacific Ocean.

The good weather lasted just seven days. A week later, in the night of the tenth of September, a severe storm attacked the little fleet, and the next morning the ships had lost sight of one another. They came together after a short search, but during the next night there was another gale, and in the morning three of the five ships had disappeared. Only the Trouwe and the Geloof were apparently saved. During three weeks these two ships floated aimlessly about, driven hither and thither upon the angry waves of the Pacific Ocean. They had few supplies left, and they could not repair the damage that was done to their masts because both ships had sent their carpenters to one of the other vessels which had been in need of a general overhauling and which was now lost. A month went by, and then they discovered that they had been driven back into the strait. The admiral discussed the situation with his chief officers. Did they advise going back to Holland without having accomplished anything, or would they keep on? The sailors all wanted to return to Holland. They did not have any faith left in the results of this unhappy voyage. Many of them were ill. Others pretended that they were too weak to work. Others murmured about a lack of provisions. There was ground for this talk. The supply-room was getting emptier and emptier in a very mysterious way. At last the admiral decided to investigate this strange case. He discovered that an unknown member of the crew possessed a key to the bread-boxes and stuffed himself every night while his comrades were kept on short rations. It was a gross breach of discipline. Apparently the expedition was going from bad to worse. On the afternoon of the tenth of December Admiral de Weert paid a call to the Trouwe to talk over the situation. The next morning the Trouwe had disappeared. De Weert never saw her again. He was all alone, and his safe return depended upon his own unaided efforts. His first duty was to get enough food. On a certain Sunday afternoon the few men of his ship who could still walk were on shore looking for things to eat when they had an encounter with a large number of natives who had just arrived in three canoes. The natives fled, and hid themselves among the cliffs. One woman and two small babies could not get away and were brought back to the ship. The woman was kept a prisoner for forty-eight hours while the Hollanders studied the habits and customs of the wild people of Tierra del Fuego. The subject of their study refused to eat cooked food, but dead birds which were thrown to her she ate as if she had been a wild animal. The children did the same thing, tearing at the feathers with their sharp teeth. After two days the mother and one of the children were sent back to the shore with a number of presents. The other child was kept on board and was taken back to Holland, where it died immediately after arrival. On the sixteenth of December a last attempt was made to find the Trouwe. A blank cartridge was fired, and a few minutes later a distant answer was heard. Soon a ship came sailing around a nearby cape. It was not the Trouwe, but the ship of Oliver van Noort, who at the head of his expedition had just entered upon the last stretch of his voyage through the strait. Van Noort had a story to tell of a fairly successful voyage, plenty to eat, and little illness. The hungry men of De Weert looked with envy at the happy faces of Van Noort's sailors. The latter had just caught several thousand penguins on a little island not far away. The starving crew of the Geloof asked that they be allowed to sail to this island and catch whatever Van Noort had left alive. De Weert, however, refused this request. Here was his last chance to get to the Indies in the company of the squadron of Van Noort, and he meant to take it. The next morning he joined the new ships on their westward course. But his sailors, weak and miserable after more than a year of illness, could not obey their captain's commands as fast as those who were on the other ships. Soon the Geloof was left behind. The next morning, when Van Noort entered the Pacific, De Weert was helplessly blown back into the strait. It seemed impossible to do more than he had tried to accomplish against such great odds. He called all his remaining sailors together to hear what they wanted him to do. They all had just one wish, to get home as fast as possible by way of Brazil and Africa. The Pacific, so they argued, offered nothing but disappointment. De Weert promised to give his final decision on the next day, which was the first of January of the year 1600. When the morning came, he found himself once more in the company of other ships. Van Noort had reached the Pacific, but the Western storms had been too much for his strong ships. For the second time the Hollanders were all united in a cold little harbor inside the Strait of Magellan.

Van Noort now paid a personal visit to De Weert and asked what he could do to help him. De Weert was much obliged for this offer, and asked for bread enough to last him another four months. Unfortunately Van Noort could not do this. He had still a very long voyage before him, and did not dare to deprive his own men of their supplies. He advised De Weert to go to the island of the penguins and to fill his storeroom with the dried meat of these birds. Meanwhile, much to his regret, he must leave De Weert as soon as possible, for he was in a hurry.

The next day they said farewell to one another for the last time. De Weert took the precautions to leave instructions for the captain of the lost Trouwe. He wrote a letter which was placed inside a bottle, and this bottle was buried at the foot of a high tree. On the tree itself a board was hammered, and on this board a message was painted telling in Dutch where to look for an important document at the foot of the tree. Then the ship sailed to the penguin island, and the thirty men who could do any work at all hunted the fat and lazy birds until they had killed several thousand. It was easy work.

The penguins obligingly waited on their nests until they were killed. But the trip to the island almost destroyed the entire expedition. There was only one boat left, and in this boat the men who were not sick had rowed to the shore. They had been careless in fastening her, and a sudden squall caught her and threw her on the rocks. She was badly damaged and could not be used without being repaired, but the men on shore had no tools with which to do any repairing, while those on the ship were so ill that they could not swim to the shore with the necessary hammers and saws. Two entire days were used to get that boat into order with the help of one ax and some pocket-knives, and during those two days the men lived out in the open on the cold shore and lived on raw penguin meat.

The island, among other things, contained material evidences of Van Noort's presence. A dead native, with his hands tied behind his back, was found stretched out upon the sand. In a little hollow in the rocks they discovered a woman who had been wounded by a gunshot. They took good care of the woman, bandaged her wounds, and gave her a pocket-knife. To show her gratitude, she told De Weert of another island where there were even more penguins. The next week was spent on this island, and now the men had plenty of food. But the ship was without a single anchor and had only one leaking lifeboat. With the certainty that he could not land anywhere unless boats were sent for him from shore De Weert decided to return to the coast of Guinea and try to reach home. On the eighteenth of January the Geloof went back upon her track. Two months later the vessel reached the coast of Guinea. This trip back was not very eventful except for one small incident. One of the sailors who was a drunkard had broken into the storeroom and had stolen a lot of rice and several bottles of wine. Theft was one of the things which was punished most severely. Therefore, the man had been condemned to death and was to be hanged. But while he was sitting in the rigging and waiting for somebody to push him into eternity the other members of the crew felt sorry for him and asked their captain to spare his life. At first he refused, but finally he agreed to show clemency if the men would never bother him again with a similar request. The prisoner was allowed to come down from his high perch, and to show his gratitude he broke again into the storeroom that same night. He was a very bad example. As such he was hanged from the yardarm of the highest mast, and his body was dropped into the sea.

The crew, however, were so thoroughly demoralized by this time that even such drastic measures did no good. They continued to pillage the storeroom, and when at last four of them had been detected and had been found guilty, their comrades were so weak that nobody could be found to hang the prisoners properly and they had to be taken home.

In July of the year 1600 the Geloof reached the English Channel, and on the thirteenth of that month she entered the mouth of the Maas. There, within sight of home, one more sailor died. He was number sixty-nine. Only thirty-six men came back to Rotterdam. They were ill and had a story to tell of constant hardships and of terrible disappointments. The great expedition of the two courageous merchants and all their investments were a complete loss. None of the other ships ever came back to Holland. But year after year stragglers from the other four ships reached home and told of the fate of the other three hundred sailors who had taken part in the unfortunate voyage. Some of these reports have come down to us, and we are able to give a short account of the adventures of each ship after that day early in the year 1600 when the Pacific storms had separated them from one another.

First of all there was the Trouwe, which had remained faithful to De Weert after the other three vessels had disappeared. The wind had blown the Trouwe out of the strait into the Pacific Ocean. For many weeks her captain had lost all track of his whereabouts. Through sheer luck he had at last reached a coast which he supposed to be the continent of South America and after a search of a few days he had found some natives who were friendly. The natives told the Hollanders that this was not the American continent, but an island called Chiloe, situated a few miles off the Chilean coast. The Dutch ships had been made welcome. They were invited to stay in the harbor as long as they wished. Meanwhile the natives told their captain about a plan of their own which undoubtedly would please him. It seemed that the inhabitants of Chiloe had good reason to hate the Spaniards, who were mighty on the near-by continent and who recently had built a strong fort on the island, from which they exercised their tyrannical rule over all the natives and made them pay very heavy tribute. Perhaps, so the natives argued, the Hollanders could be induced to give their assistance in a campaign against the Spaniard. De Cordes, who commanded the Trouwe, was a Catholic, but he was quite ready to offer his services in so good a cause and was delighted to start a little private war of his own upon the Spaniards. He made ready to sail for that part of the coast where, according to his informants, the Spaniard had fortified himself. Meanwhile the natives were to proceed on shore toward the same Spanish fortress. An attack was to follow simultaneously from the land and the sea. On the way to the fortress all Spanish houses and plantations, storerooms and churches, were burned down and at last the fortress itself was reached. The commander of the fortress, however, had heard of the approach of this handful of Hollanders, and he sent them an insulting message telling them that he needed a new stable boy, anyway, and would bestow this high office upon the Dutch captain as soon as he could have the necessary arrangements made. But when the Dutch captain actually appeared upon the scene with a well-armed vessel and a band of native auxiliaries and informed the Spaniard that the new stable boy had come to take possession of his domain, the commander changed his mind and offered the Hollanders whatever they wished if they would only leave him alone. De Cordes, however, attacked the fort at once. He took it, and the garrison was locked up in the church as prisoners. Then the Chilean natives in their rage attacked the church and killed several of the Spaniards. This was not what De Cordes wanted to be done. He did not mind if a Hollander killed a Spaniard, but it did not look well for one white man to allow a native to kill another while he himself stood by. Therefore he returned their arms to the Spaniards and together they then drove the natives away. When the natives, however, told the Dutch sailors that the fort contained hidden treasures of which the Spaniards had made no mention, the former allies attacked each other for the second time, and the Spanish prisoners were sent on board the Dutch ship. The story which we possess of this episode of the voyage is not very clear. It was written many years later by one of the few sailors who came back to Holland. His account of these adventures was so badly printed and the spelling of the original pamphlet was so extraordinary that a second scribe was later hired to turn the booklet into more or less readable Dutch. The present translation has been made from this second version. Everything is a bit mixed, and it is not easy to find out what really happened. A common and ignorant sailor of the year 1600 was not very different from the same sort of fellow who at present is fighting in the European war. They both remember events in chunks, so to speak. They have very vivid impressions of a few occurrences, but they have forgotten other things of more importance because at the time these did not strike their unobservant brain as being of any special interest. But we have no other account of the adventures of the Trouwe. We must use this information such as it is.

The booty found in this small settlement had not been of great value. The expedition felt inclined to move toward a richer port. They did not have food enough for their prisoners, and fourteen of the nineteen Spaniards who were locked up in the hold were thrown overboard. This sounds very cruel, but it was the custom of the time that these two nations rarely gave each other quarter. Whosoever was made a prisoner was killed. The Spaniards started this practice in the middle of the sixteenth century because the Hollanders as heretics deserved no better fate. The Hollanders reciprocated. On this distant island of the Pacific both parties obeyed the unwritten law. The Hollanders drowned their prisoners. When Spanish reinforcements reached Chiloe and retook the fort, they killed the Dutch garrison, for such was the custom of the time.

The Trouwe after this famous exploit was in a difficult position, all alone in the heart of the Pacific, with enemies on every side and a bad conscience. The idea of attacking some other Spanish harbor in Chile and Peru was given up as too dangerous. Near the harbor of Truxillo a Spanish ship loaded with grain and wine was captured, and provided with new supplies, De Cordes decided to risk the trip across the Pacific. On the third of January, 1601, he reached Ternate in the Indies, where Van Noort had been the year before, and where they found a Dutch settlement commanded by that same Van der Does whose account of Houtman's first trip to India we have given in the fourth chapter of this little book. Van der Does warned De Cordes not to visit the next island of Tidore. There were only twenty-four Hollanders left on board the Trouwe. It was too dangerous to visit an unfriendly Portuguese colony with a damaged ship and so small a crew. But De Cordes, who seems to have been a reckless sort of person, went to Tidore all the same. Much to his surprise he was very cordially received by the commander of the Portuguese garrison and the governor of the town. They both assured him that he might trade in their colony as much as he wished. If, however, he would let them know what he wished to buy, they would give orders that provisions and a cargo of spice should be got ready for their distinguished visitors. They invited him to come on shore the next morning. They wanted to make him a present of an ox for the benefit of his hungry crew and entertain him personally, and, then after a few more days further arrangements for the purpose of a mutually profitable trade might be made. The next morning the Dutch captain and six men went ashore to get their ox. The ship itself was left in the care of the first mate. Soon a Portuguese boat rowed out to the Trouwe and asked the mate to come on shore, too, and have breakfast with his Portuguese colleagues. The mate was suspicious and refused the invitation. He suggested that the Portuguese officer come on board the Trouwe and breakfast with him. But the officer said that he was too heavy a man to climb on board so high a ship, and he did not care to take this exercise so early in the morning. So the mate left the ship, together with the ship's carpenter, to see what a Portuguese kitchen served for breakfast. The moment the two men landed a loud outcry was heard from the Trouwe. The mate at once jumped into the sea and looked for his comrade. The carpenter was dead and his head, hacked from his body, was used as a football by the Portuguese. The mate swam out to the ship, but when he reached it he found that the Portuguese had jumped on board the moment he had left for his breakfast party. He swam back to the shore, was made a prisoner, and was locked up in the fortress. With six other men he escaped the general murder which had taken place as soon as he landed. De Cordes himself had been killed with a dagger. The six men who had accompanied him on shore had heard the noise of the attack upon the Trouwe and had rowed away from shore in a boat, trying to get back to their vessel. But the Trouwe was already in the hands of the Portuguese, and since the Hollanders had no arms, they surrendered after the Portuguese had given their oath not to hurt them and to spare their lives. They were taken on board a Portuguese ship. As soon as they were on deck they had been placed in a row, and a soldier had been ordered to take his sword and hack their heads off. He had killed four men when the other two managed to jump overboard. One of these was drowned. The other was fished out of the water and was sent to the fortress with the mate and five sailors who had put up such a desperate fight on board the Trouwe that the Portuguese had promised to treat them with clemency if only they would surrender.

The six men were afterward taken to Goa. Gradually one after the other they had managed to escape and find their way back to Holland. Two of them returned to Rotterdam in the autumn of 1603. Another one we find mentioned in later years as commander of an Indian trader. As for the Trouwe, Van Neck on his second voyage to India found the vessel being used by the Portuguese as a man-of-war.

Of the other ships, the Blyde Boodschap also had a very sad career and met with extraordinary adventures. This small vessel was commanded by a certain Dirck Gerritsz, a native of Enkhuizen, a fellow-citizen of Linschoten. As a matter of fact the two men had heard of each other many years before. While Linschoten was in Goa he was told of a Hollander who was a native of his own city and who had traveled not only in the Indies, but who also had visited Japan and China. We know very little of the man. Some information of his travels in Asia have been printed in a general hand-book on navigation of that time, though he did not follow Linschoten's example and print a full account of his adventures. When the city of Rotterdam sent this expedition to the Strait of Magellan, Dirck Gerritsz had been engaged as first mate of the Blyde Boodschap. When her captain died he had succeeded him. The ship of Gerritsz had suffered from the same storm which had driven the Trouwe out of her course. An attempt had been made to reach the island of *Santa Maria*, but the maps on board proved to be faulty, and the little island could not be found. With only provisions enough for another week Gerritsz had finally reached the harbor of Valparaiso. Of his original crew of fifty-six men, twenty-three were left, and of these only nine were strong enough to sail the ship. Therefore he had been forced to surrender himself and his vessel to the Spaniards. The Dutch sailors were forced to take service in the Spanish navy. From that moment on we lose sight of all of them. A few reached home after many years of strange adventure. Others died in the Spanish service. Of the fate of the ship we know nothing. As for Dirck Gerritsz, rumor has it that he found his way back to Enkhuizen.

There were two other ships, the Hoop and the Liefde. Of these the Liefde had reached *Santa Maria*, and after leaving the island had landed at Punta Lapavia, where an attempt had been made to find fresh water. Unfortunately, the captain and twenty-three of his men had been murdered by natives who mistook them for Spaniards and had carried their heads in triumph to the Spanish town of Concepcion, where they were shown to the garrison as a promise of what was in store for them should the settlement ever fall into the hands of the enraged native population. The rest of the sailors had saved their ship by fleeing to *Santa Maria*, where they met the Hoop. The Hoop had suffered a similar calamity. Her captain and twenty-seven of his men had been murdered on another island. Of the officers of both ships hardly a single one was still alive.

New officers were elected from among the men, and the ships continued their northward course apparently without a definite idea of what they intended to do. They could not go back through the strait, and they were obliged to cross the Pacific. They decided to avoid all Spanish and Portuguese settlements and to make for Japan, where they might be able to sell their cargo, and where a peaceful couple of ships might find it possible to do some honest trading without being attacked by wild natives or lying Spaniards. On the twenty-seventh of November the island of *Santa Maria* was left, and soon the ships passed the equator. They kept near the land, and lost eight more of their men when these had gone to the shore to get fresh water and were attacked by natives. On the twenty-third of February, during a gale, the ships were separated from each other. The Liefde was obliged to make the voyage to Japan alone. On the twenty-fourth of March of the year 1600 the first Japanese island was reached.

The people of Japan were very kind-hearted and very obliging. The sick Hollanders were allowed to come on shore, and the others could trade as much as they liked. But Japan for many years had been a field of successful activities for Portuguese Jesuits. These Jesuits smiled pleasantly upon the Dutch visitors, but to the Japanese they hinted that the Hollanders were pirates and could not be trusted. Holland was not a country at all, and these men were all robbers and thieves. They advised the Japanese authorities to let these dangerous people starve or send them away from their island, which would mean the same thing. But the news of the arrival of some strange ships had reached the ears of the Emperor of Japan. He sent for some of the crew to come to his court. An Englishman among the sailors by the name of William Adams was chosen for this dangerous mission. He not only represented to his imperial Majesty the sad state of affairs among the shipwrecked Hollanders, but he made himself so useful at the imperial court that he was asked to remain behind and serve the Japanese state. He had a wife and children at home in England, but he liked this new country so well that he decided to stay. He lived happily for twenty years, married a Japanese woman, and when he died in 1620 divided his fortune equally among his Japanese and his English families.

Without the assistance of Adams, who seems to have been the leader of the remaining sailors on the Liefde, it was impossible to accomplish anything with the big ship. Of the twenty-four men who had reached Japan only eighteen were left. The ship, therefore, was deserted, and all the men went on shore. Except for two, the others all disappeared from view. They probably settled down in Japan. But in the year 1605, in the month of December, two Hollanders came to the Dutch settlement of Patani, on the Indian peninsula. They had made the voyage from Japan to India on a Japanese ship, and they brought to the Dutch company trading in that region an official invitation from the Emperor of Japan asking them to come and enter into honorable commerce with the Japanese islands. This invitation was accepted. In the year 1608 one of the two Dutch messengers returned to Japan with letters announcing the arrival of a Dutch fleet for the next summer. He continued to live in Japan until his death in 1634. The other sailor found a chance to go back to Holland on a Dutch ship, but near home he was killed in a quarrel with some Portuguese. The net result of this unfortunate voyage of the Liefde was the establishment of a very useful trade relation with Japan—a relation which became more important after the Portuguese had been expelled, and which lasted for over two centuries.

Finally there was the ship called the Hoop, which had become separated from the Liefde on the coast of South America in February of the year 1600. It went down to the bottom of the ocean with everybody on board.

CHAPTER VIII
THE BAD LUCK OF CAPTAIN BONTEKOE

Captain Bontekoe was a pious man who sailed the ocean in command of several Dutch ships during the early part of the seventeenth century. He never did anything remarkable as a navigator, he never discovered a new continent or a new strait or even a new species of bird but he was blown up with his ship, flew heavenward, landed in the ocean, and survived this experience to tell a tale of such harrowing bad luck that the compassionate world read his story for over three centuries with tearful eyes. Wherefore we shall copy as much as is desirable from his famous diary, which was published in the year 1647.

On the twenty-eighth of December of the year 1618, William Ysbrantsz Bontekoe, with a

ship of 550 ton and 206 men, left the roads of Texel for India. The name of the vessel was the Nieuw Hoorn, and it was loaded with gunpowder. Kindly remember that gunpowder. There were the usual storms, the usual broken masts; the customary number of sick sailors either died or recovered; the customary route along the coast of Africa was followed. The weather, once the cape was left behind, was fine, and a short stay on the island of Reunion allowed the sick to regain their health and the dead to be buried. The natives were well disposed and traded with Bontekoe. They entertained him and danced for the amusement of his men, and everything was as happy as could be.

At last the voyage across the Indian Ocean was started under the best of auspices, and the Nieuw Hoorn had almost reached the Strait of Sunda when the great calamity occurred. On the nineteenth of November, almost a year, therefore, after the ship had left Holland, one of the pantrymen went into the hold to get himself some brandy. It was very dark in the hold, and therefore he had taken a candle with him. This candle, in a short iron holder, with a sharp point to it, he stuck into a barrel which was on top of the one out of which he filled his bottle. When he got through with his job he jerked the iron candlestick out of the wood of the barrel. In doing so a small piece of burning tallow fell into the brandy. That caused an explosion, and the next moment the brandy inside the barrel had caught fire. Fortunately there were two pails of water standing near by, and the fire was easily extinguished. A lot more water was pumped upon the dangerous barrels, and the fire, as far as anybody could see or smell, had been put out. But half an hour later the dreadful cry of "Fire!" was heard once more all through the ship. This time the coals which were in the hold near the brandy, and which were used for the kitchen stove and the blacksmith shop, had caught fire. They filled the hold with poisonous gas and a thick and yellowish smoke. For the second time the pumps were set to work to fill the hold with water. But the air inside the hold was so bad that the firemen had a difficult task. As the hours went by the fire grew worse. Bontekoe proposed to throw his cargo of gunpowder overboard. But as I have related in my first chapters, there always was a civilian commander on board such Indian vessels. It was his duty to look after the cargo and to represent the commercial interest of the company. Bontekoe's civilian master did not wish to lose his valuable gunpowder. He told the captain to leave it where it was and try to put out the fire. Bontekoe obeyed, but soon his men could no longer stand the smoke in the hold. Large holes were then hacked through the deck and through these water was poured upon the cargo. Now Bontekoe was a pious man, but he was neither very strong of character nor very resourceful of mind. He spent his time in running about the ship giving many orders, the majority of which were to no great purpose. Meanwhile he did not notice that part of the crew, from fear of being blown up, had lowered the boats and were getting ready to leave the ship. The civilian director, who had just told the captain to save the gunpowder, had been the first to join in the flight. He was soon safely riding the waves in a small boat far away from the doomed ship.

For those who had been deserted on board there was only one way to salvation; they must try to put out the fire or be killed. Under personal command of their captain they set to work and pumped and pumped and pumped. But the fire had reached several barrels of oil, and there was a dense smoke. It was impossible to throw 310 barrels of powder overboard in the suffocating atmosphere of the hold, yet the men tried to do it. They worked with desperate speed, but before the sixth part of the dangerous cargo was in the waters of the ocean the fire reached the forward part, where the powder was stored. A few moments later one hundred and ninety men were blown skyward, together with pieces of the masts and pieces of the ship and heavy iron bars and pieces of sail and everything that belongs to a well-equipped vessel. "And I, Captain Willem Ysbrantsz Bontekoe, commander of the ship, also flew through the sky, and I thought that my end had come. So I stretched my hands and arms toward heaven and said: 'O dear Lord, there I go! Please have pity upon this miserable sinner!' because I thought that now the next moment I must be dead; but all the time I was flying through the air I kept my mind clear, and I found that there was happiness in my heart; yes, I even found that I was quite gay, and so came down again, and landed in the water between pieces of the ship which had been blown into little scraps."

This is the captain's own minute account of the psychology of being blown up. He continues:

"And when I was now once in the water of the sea, I felt my courage return in such a way that it was as if I had become a new man. And when I looked around I found a piece of the mainmast floating at my side, and so I climbed on top of it, and looking over the scene around me, I said, 'O Lord, so hath this fine ship been destroyed even as Sodom and Gomorrah.'"

For a short while the skipper floated and contemplated upon his mast, and then he noticed that he was no longer alone. A young German who had been on board as a common sailor came swimming to the wreckage. He climbed on the only piece of the ship's stern that was afloat, and pulling the captain's mast nearer to him with a long stick which he had fished out of the water, he helped our good Bontekoe to pull himself on board his wreckage. There they were together on the lonely ocean on a few boards and with no prospect of rescue. Both the boats were far away, and showed themselves only as small black dots upon the distant horizon. Bontekoe told his comrade to pray with him. For a long time they whispered their supplications to heaven. Then they looked once more to see what the boats were doing. And behold! their prayer had been answered. The boats came rowing back as fast as they could. When they saw the two men they tried to reach the wreckage; but they did not dare to come too near for their heavily loaded boats ran the risk of being thrown against the remains of the hulk. In that case they would have been swamped. Bontekoe had felt very happy as long as he had been up in the air. Now, however, he began to notice that he had hurt his back badly and that he had been wounded in the head. He did not dare to swim to the boats, but the bugler of the ship, who was in the first boat, swam back to the wreckage, fastened a rope around Bontekoe's waist, and in this fashion the commander was pulled safely on board, where he was made as comfortable as could be. During the night the two boats remained near the place of the misfortune because they hoped that they might find a few things to eat in the morning. They had only a little bread and no water at all.

Meanwhile the exhausted skipper slept, and when in the morning his men told him that they had nothing to eat he was very angry, for the day before the sea around his mast had been full of all sorts of boxes and barrels and there had been enough to eat for everybody. During the night, however, the boats had been blown away from the wreckage by the wind. There was no chance to get anything at all. Eight pounds of bread made up the total amount of provisions for seventy strong men. Of these there were forty-six in one and twenty-six in the second boat. Part of that bread was used by the ship's doctor to make a plaster for Bontekoe's wounds. With the help of a pillow which had been found in the locker of the biggest boat and which he wore around his head, Bontekoe was then partly restored to life, and he took command of his squadron and decided what ought to be done. There were masts in the boat, but the sails had been forgotten. Therefore he ordered the men to give up their shirts. Out of these, two large sails were made. They were primitive sails, but they caught the breeze, and with the help of the western wind Bontekoe hoped to reach the coast of Sumatra, which, according to the best guess of all those on board, must be seventy miles to the east. All those who had the map of that part of India fairly well in their heads were consulted, and upon a piece of wood a chart of the coast of Sumatra, the Sunda Islands, and the west coast of Java was neatly engraved with the help of a nail and a pocket-knife. A few simple instruments were cut out of old planks, and the curious expedition was ready to navigate further eastward.

Fortunately it rained very hard during the first night. The sails made out of shirts were used to catch the rain, and the water was carefully saved in two small empty barrels which had been found in one of the two boats. A drinking-cup was cut out of a wooden stopper, and each of the sailors in turn got a few drops of water. For many hours they sailed, and they became dreadfully hungry. Again a merciful Heaven came to their assistance. A number of sea-gulls came flying around the boats, and many of them ventured so near that they seemed to say "Please catch us." Of course they were caught and killed, and although there was no way of cooking them, they were eaten by the hungry men as fast as they came. But a sea-gull is not a very fat bird, and again there was hunger, and not yet any sight of land. The big boat was a good sailor, but the small one could not keep up with her. Therefore the men in the small boat asked that they might be taken on board the big one, so that they might either perish together or all be saved. The sailors in the large boat did not like the idea. They feared that their boat could not hold all of the seventy-six men. After a while, however, they gave in. The men from the small boat were taken on board. Out of the extra oars a sort of deck was rigged up on top of the boat, and under this a number of the men were allowed to sleep while the others sat on top and looked for land or prayed for food and water.

No further sea-gulls came to feed this forlorn expedition, but just when they were so hungry that they could not stand it any longer, large shoals of flying-fish suddenly jumped out of the water into the boats. Again the men were saved. The two little barrels of water had been emptied by this time. For the second time the men expected that they would all perish. They sailed eastward, but they saw no land, and finally they got so hungry and thirsty that they talked about killing the cabin boy and eating him. Bontekoe asked them please not to do it, and he prayed the good Lord not to allow this horrible thing to happen. The men, however, said that they were very hungry and must have something to eat. Then he asked that they should wait just three days more. If no land was seen after three days, they might eat the cabin boy.

On the thirteenth day after the explosion there was a severe thunder-storm, and the barrels were filled with fresh water. Most of the men then crept under the little cover to be out of the rain, and only one of the mates was left on deck. It was very hazy, but when the fog parted for a moment he saw land very near the boat. The next morning the survivors reached an uninhabited island, where there was no fresh water, but an abundance of cocoanut-trees. The men attacked these cocoanuts with such greedy hunger and they drank the sap with such haste that on the succeeding day they were all very ill, with great pains and a feeling that they might explode at any moment just as their ship had done.

From the presence of this island Bontekoe argued that the coast of Sumatra must be about fifteen miles distant. He filled the boat with many cocoanuts, a wonderful fruit because it is food and drink at the same time, and sailed farther eastward. After seventy hours he actually reached Sumatra, but the surf did not allow him to land at once. It took an entire day before his men managed to row through that terrible surf, and then only at the cost of a swamped boat. At last, however, they did reach the shore, bailed out their boat, and made a fire to dry their clothes and to rest from the fatigue of this terrible experience. Some of the sailors meanwhile explored the country near by, and to their great astonishment they found the ashes of an old fire and near it some tobacco. This was very welcome, for the men had not smoked for many weeks. They also found some beans. These they ate so greedily that they were all ill, and in the middle of the night, when they lay around groaning and moaning, they were suddenly attacked by the natives of the island. They had no arms, but they defended themselves as well as possible with sticks and pieces of burning wood which they picked up out of the fire. The natives fled, and the next morning sent three messengers to have a talk with the shipwrecked Hollanders. They wanted to know why he and his men had come to their island. They were told the story of the burning ship and the explosion which had killed many of the other sailors. Bontekoe said that he was a peaceful traveler, and would pay for everything he bought. The natives believed this story, and came back with chickens and rice and all sorts of eatables, for which Bontekoe paid with money. The natives then told him that this land was Sumatra and that Java was a little farther to the east. They even knew the name of the governor-general, and Bontekoe now felt certain that he was on the right road to a Dutch harbor.

Before he left he made a little trip up the river to buy more food, for he counted upon a long voyage in the small boat. This visit almost cost him his life. One day he had bought a carabao. He had paid for the animal, and told the four sailors who were with him to bring it to the camp; but the carabao was so wild that they could not manage it. The four sailors decided to spend the night in the village and try their luck once more the next morning. Bontekoe thought that this was too dangerous, and when his men refused to return to join the others, he hired two natives to paddle him back in their own canoe. The natives told him the price for which they would row him back to the camp, and he gave them the required sum; but when they were out in the middle of the river they threatened to kill Bontekoe unless he gave them more money. Bontekoe said a short prayer and felt very uncomfortable. Then he heard a voice inside himself tell him to sing a funny song. This he did. He sang so loud that the noise resounded through the quiet forests on both sides of the river. The two natives thought that this was the funniest thing that they had ever heard, and they laughed so uproariously that they forgot all about their plan to kill the white man, and Bontekoe came safely back to his own people.

The next morning a number of natives appeared with a carabao, but Bontekoe saw at once that it was not the same one that he had bought the day before. He asked about it, and wanted to know where his men were. "Oh," the natives said, "they are lazy and they will come a little later." This looked suspicious, but whatever happened, Bontekoe must have his carabao to be eaten on the trip across the Strait of Sunda. Therefore he tried to kill the animal, but when they saw this the natives suddenly began to call him names and they shrieked until several hundred others came running from the bushes and attacked the Hollanders. These fled back to their boat, but before they could reach it eleven men had been killed. Of those who scrambled on board one had been hit in the stomach with a poisoned arrow. Bontekoe performed an operation, trying to cut away the flesh around the wound, but he did not succeed in saving the life of the poor fellow. There were now only fifty-six men left.

With only eight chickens for so many men Bontekoe did not dare to cross the strait. The next morning, armed, he went on shore, and, having gathered a lot of clams and filled the small barrels with fresh water, sailed away for the coast of Java. They sailed all day long, but at night there came so violent a wind that the sails had to be taken down, and the boat drifted whither it pleased the good Lord to send it. It pleased Him to bring it the next morning near three small islands densely covered with palm-trees. Out of the bamboo which grew near the shore several water-barrels were improvised. There was still some food, but not much. Therefore the discovery of these islands did not bring much relief to the poor shipwrecked people. Bontekoe wandered about in a despondent mood, and when he saw a small hill he climbed to the top of it to be alone and to pray to the good Lord for his divine counsel. He prayed for a long time, and when at last he opened his eyes he saw that the clouds on the horizon had parted and that there was more land in the distance, and out of this he saw two bluish-looking mountains lifting their peaks. Suddenly he remembered that his friend, Captain Schouten, who had been in those parts of India, had often told him of two strange blue mountains which he had often seen in Java. He had sailed across the sea which separated Sumatra from Java, and the island on which he and his men now were was a little island off the coast of Java. He knew his way now, and he ordered his men to row as fast as they could. A boy was told to climb the mast and keep watch. And, behold! the next day the sailors suddenly saw a large Dutch fleet of twenty-three ships, under Frederik Houtman, who had left Texel with Bontekoe and was on his way to Batavia. He took all the men on board his ships. He fed them, gave them clothes, and carried them to Batavia, the newly founded capital of the Dutch East Indies, where the governor general, one Jan Pieterszoon Coen, received them very kindly, and appointed Bontekoe to be captain of a new ship, of thirty-two guns, which plied between the different colonies and carried provisions and supplies of war from Java to the other colonies. It also brought to Java the granite which was necessary to build the strong fort where the government of the colony was to reside. Later on Bontekoe was made captain of another ship called the Groningen, and he visited China, where the Dutch company tried to capture the Portuguese colony in Macao and to build a fort on one of the Pescadores Islands to protect their Chinese trade.

After two years of this work Bontekoe wanted to return home, and he asked to be given the command of a ship that was about to leave for Holland. He was given command of the Hollandia, which with two other ships left Batavia on the sixth of February of the year of our Lord 1625. But Bontekoe's bad luck had not yet come to an end. This patient man, who never lost his temper and accepted everything that happened to him with devout resignation, once more became the victim of all sorts of unfortunate occurrences. On the nineteenth of March his ship was attacked by a terrible storm, and soon the waves threatened to swamp the vessel. Bontekoe ordered the men to work the pumps as hard as they could. Then the pepper stowed away in the hold broke loose, got into the pumps and clogged them. Finally baskets were placed about the lower part of the pumps to keep the pernicious pepper out of them, and the Hollandia was saved.

Of the other two ships, one, the Gouda, had disappeared when the morning came, and the other, the Middelburg, had suffered much. Her masts were broken, and they had no spare the Atlantic. Finally the Middelburg left part of his spare yards for masts, and then he sailed with all possible haste for Madagascar to repair his own damage. He reached the island inside a week, and cut himself a mast out of a tree. He repaired his ship and spent a month on the island, where he was well received by the natives, who flocked from all over to see how the Hollanders made a new ship out of the wreck which they had saved from the storm. Here Bontekoe waited for the other ships. But the Gouda had sunk, and the other, the Middelburg, reached Madagascar much later, and spent several months in the bay of Antongil. Most of her people were ill and among those who died on the island was the commander of the ship, Willem Schouten, who with Le Maire had discovered the new route between the Pacific and the Atlantic. Finally the Middleburg left Madagascar and sailed to St. Helena. There she got into a fight with two Portuguese vessels, and that is the last word we have ever received of her. As for Bontekoe, he, too, reached St. Helena, where he wanted to take in fresh water. But a Spanish ship had landed troops, and he was not allowed to come on shore. So he went farther on, and at last reached Kinsale in Ireland. This time the joys of life on land almost finished the brave captain who so often had escaped the anger of the waves. His sailors went on shore, and after the long voyage they appreciated the hospitality of the Irish inns so well that they refused to come back on board. They stayed on shore until the mayor of the city, at the request of Bontekoe, forbade the owners of ale-houses to give the Hollanders more than seven shillings' credit apiece. As soon as this was known the men, many of whom had spent much more than that, hastened back to their ship. Crowds of furious innkeepers and their wives, crying aloud for their money, followed them.

Good Captain Bontekoe paid everybody what he or she had a right to ask, and finally, on the twenty-fifth of November of the year 1625, he reached home. Bontekoe went to live quietly in his native city of Hoorn. He had written a short account of his voyage, but he had never printed it because he did not think that he could write well enough. But one of his fellow-townsmen wanted to write a large volume upon the noble deeds of the people of Hoorn, and he asked Bontekoe to write down the main events of his famous voyage, and he promised to edit the little book for the benefit of the reading public.

And behold! this same public, saturated with stories of wild men and wild animals and terrible storms and uninhabited islands and treacherous Portuguese and hairbreadth escapes, took such a fancy to the simple recital of Bontekoe's pious trip toward heaven and the patience with which he had accepted the vicissitudes of life that they read his little book long after the more ponderous volumes had been left to the kind ministrations of the meritorious book-worm.

CHAPTER IX SCHOUTEN AND LE MAIRE DISCOVER A NEW STRAIT

This is the story of a voyage to a country which did not exist. The men who risked their capital in this expedition hoped to reach a territory which we now call Australia. It was not exactly the Australia which we know from our modern geography. It was a mysterious continent of which there had been heard many rumors for more than half a century. What the contemporary traveler really hoped to find we do not know, but we have the details of an expedition to this new land called "Terra Australis incognita" or "the unknown southern land," an expedition which left the harbor of Hoorn on the fifteenth of June of the year 1615.

Hoorn is a little city on the Zuyder Zee, just such a little city as Enkhuizen, from which Linschoten had set out upon his memorable voyage. This voyage had a short preface which has little to do with navigation, but much with provincial politics and commercial rivalry. The original idea of allowing everybody to found his own little Indian trading company after his own wishes had been a bad one from an economic point of view. There was so much competition between the three dozen little companies that all were threatened with bankruptcy. Therefore a financial genius, the eminent leader of the province of Holland, John of Barneveldt, took matters into his own capable hands and combined all the little companies into one large East India Trading Company, a commercial body which existed until the year 1795 and was a great success from start to finish.

Among the original investors there had been a certain Jacques le Maire, a native of the town of Antwerp who had fled when the Spaniards took that city for the second time, and who now lived in Amsterdam with his wife and his twenty-two children. He was respected for his ability, and was chosen into the body of directors who managed the affairs of the East India Company. But Le Maire was not the sort of man to stay in the harness with others for a very long time. He complained that the company cared only for dividends and immediate profits. He wanted to see the ships of his adopted country make war upon the Spaniards, besides trying to steal their colonies.

After a few years Le Maire quarreled openly with several of the other directors, and he planned to form an Indian company of his own. In Amsterdam, however, he was so strongly opposed by his enemies, who were still in the old company, that he was forced to leave the city. He went to live in a small village near by and continued to work upon his schemes. With Hendrik Hudson he discussed a plan of reaching the Indies by way of the Northwestern Route—a route which was as yet untried. To King Henry IV of France he made the offer of establishing a new French company as a rival of the mighty Dutch institution. All these many ideas came to nothing. Henry IV was murdered, and Hudson went into the service of another employer.

Le Maire was obliged to invent something new. He was in a very difficult position. The Estates General of the Dutch Republic had given to their one East India Company a practical monopoly of the entire Indian trade. They decided that no Dutch ships should be allowed to travel to the Indies except through the Strait of Magellan or by way of the Cape of Good Hope. That meant that the entrance to the Indian spice islands was closed at both sides. It was of course easy enough to sail through the strait or past the cape. There was nobody to prevent one from doing so. But when one tried to trade in India on his own account, the Dutch company sent their men-of-war after the intruder. These wanted to know who he was and how he came within the domain of the company. Since there were only two roads, he must have trespassed in one way or the other upon the privileges of the company. Therefore the company, which was the sovereign ruler of all the Indian islands, had the right to confiscate his ships.

If Le Maire could only find a new road to India, he would not interfere with the strict rules of the Estates General. His ships could then trade in the Pacific and in the Indian Ocean, and he would be the most dangerous rival of the old company, which he had learned to hate since the days when he had first invested sixty thousand guilders and had been one of the directors. For a long time Le Maire studied books and maps and atlases, and finally came to the conclusion that there must be another way of getting from the Atlantic into the Pacific besides the long and tortuous Strait of Magellan. And if there were a strait, there must be land on the other side of it. If only this could be discovered, Le Maire would be rich again, and could laugh at the pretentions of the East India Company.

Le Maire did not go to Amsterdam to get the necessary funds for his expedition. He interested the good people of the little town of Hoorn, and with a fine prospectus about his "Unknown Southern Land" he soon got all the money he needed. The Estates General were willing to give him all the privileges he asked for provided he did not touch the monopolies of their beloved East India Company. Even Prince Maurice interested himself sufficiently in this voyage to a new continent to give Le Maire a letter of introduction which put the expedition upon more official footing.

Two small ships were bought, and eighty-seven men were engaged for two years. On the largest ship of the two, called the Eendracht, there were sixty-five men, and on the small yacht the Hoorn there were twenty-two. William Cornelisz Schouten was commander-in-chief. He had made three trips to India by way of the cape. Two sons of Le Maire, one called Jacques, the other Daniel, went with the expedition to keep a watchful eye upon everything and to see to it that their father's wishes were carefully executed. The ships were forbidden to enter the Strait of Magellan. In case of need they might return by way of the Cape, but they must be careful not to trade with any of the Indian princes who now recognized the rule of the East India Company. The main purpose of the expedition was to find the unknown continent in the Pacific. For this main purpose they must sacrifice everything else. And so they left Hoorn, and they sailed toward the south.

It was more than twenty years since the first expedition had sailed for India. The route across the Atlantic was well known by this time. There is nothing particular to narrate about the dull trip of three months enlivened only by the attack of a large monster, a sort of unicorn, which stuck his horn into the ship with such violence that he perished and left behind the horn, which was found when the ships were overhauled near the island of Porto Deseado, where Van Noort, too, had made ready for his trip through the strait many years before.

The cleaning of the smaller of the two vessels, however, was done so carelessly that it caught fire. Since it had been placed on a high bank at high tide and the water had ebbed, there was no water with which to extinguish the conflagration. Except for the guns, the entire ship and its contents were lost.

The sailors were taken on board the Eendracht, and on the thirteenth of January of the year 1616 the ship passed by the entrance of the Strait of Magellan and began to search for a new thoroughfare into the Pacific farther toward the South. On the twenty-third of January the most eastern promontory of Tierra del Fuego was seen. The next day the high mountains of another little island further toward the east appeared in the distance. Evidently Le Maire had been right in his calculations. There was another strait, and the Eendracht had discovered it. Such big events are usually very simple affairs. The southernmost point of Tierra del Fuego was easily reached and was called Cape Hoorn, after the town which had equipped the expedition. The Eendracht now sailed further westward, and in less than two weeks found herself in the Pacific Ocean. On the twelfth of February the great discovery was celebrated with a party for the benefit of the sailors. They had been the first to pass through the Strait of Jacques le Maire and the dangerous route discovered by Magellan ninety-five years before could now be given up for the safer and shorter passage through Strait le Maire and the open water south of Tierra del Fuego.

T'eylandt van Guan Fernando The ship had an easy voyage until it dropped its anchors before Juan Fernandez, the famous island of Robinson Crusoe. It was found to be the little paradise which De

Foe afterward painted in his entertaining novel. Fresh water was taken on board, and the voyage was continued. After a month of rapid progress, with a good eastern wind, land was seen. It was a small coral island, probably one of the Paomuta group. Some men swam ashore, for it was impossible to use the boat on account of the heavy surf. They saw nothing but a flat, naked island and three strange dogs that did not bark. They found some fresh fruit, which they brought back to the ship for the sick people. Of course there were sick people. That was a part of every voyage. But the illness was not serious. Four days later they discovered a second island somewhat larger. This was inhabited. A canoe with painted savages came out to the Dutch ship. Since the savages spoke neither Dutch, Spanish, Portuguese, nor Malay, and the Dutch sailors did not know the Papua dialect, it was impossible to have conversation with these ignorant people who refused to come on board. Captain Schouten was not in need of anything, and he went on his way to try his luck at the next island. The natives had now discovered that there was no harm in this strange, large floating object. They came climbing over all the sides of the ship. They stole brass nails and small metal objects, hid them in their wooly and long hair, and then jumped overboard. Everywhere the same thing happened. Schouten sailed from one island to the next, but of any new continent, however, he found no sign. When you look at the map you will notice that this part of the Pacific is thickly dotted with small islands. Their inhabitants are great mariners, and in their little boats travel long distances. Schouten with his big ship caused great consternation among these simple fishermen, who hastily fled whenever they saw this strange big devil bearing down upon them.

The trip was very pleasant, but it grew tiresome to discover nothing but little islands. At last, however, on the tenth of May, a big one with high mountains and forests was reached. It was called Cocos Island because there were many cocoanut-trees near the shore. The inhabitants of the island, being unfamiliar with white people, were very hospitable and were willing to trade fresh cocoanuts and other eatable things for a few gifts of trinkets and perhaps a small pocket-knife. But jealousy was not unknown even in this distant part of the South Seas. Soon there was a quarrel between those canoes nearest to the ship which had obtained presents and others too far away to receive anything. Also there was a good deal of annoyance caused by the fact that the natives insisted upon stealing everything they could find on the ship. Finally Schouten was obliged to appoint a temporary police of Hollanders armed with heavy canes to keep the natives in their proper place. Otherwise they might have stolen the ship itself, just as they had once tried to make away with all the boats. Upon that occasion they had made their first acquaintance of fire-arms. When they saw what a little bullet could do they respected the mysterious lead pipes which made a sudden loud noise and killed a man at a hundred yards. Near Cocos Island there appeared to be more mountainous land, and Schouten decided to visit it. The king came out in state in his canoe to greet the Dutch captain. He was entertained royally with a concert. To show how much he appreciated the lovely music which he had just heard the king yelled and shrieked as loudly as he could. It was very funny, and everybody was happy. But this pleasant relation did not last long, for when the Hollanders were about to reciprocate the visit their ship was attacked, and several volleys from the large cannon were necessary to drive the natives away. These islands were called the Islands of the Traitors, because the king had tried to kill the people whom he had invited as his guests, and they are known to-day as the Ladrones.

The Eendracht was now sixteen hundred miles to the west of Peru, and as yet the unknown Southern continent had not been discovered. The wind continued to blow from the east. In a council of the officers of the ship it was decided to keep a more northern course until it could be ascertained with precision where they were in this vast expanse of pacific water and small coral islands. It was an unfortunate decision. The ship was then very near the coast of Australia. Sailing from one group of islands to the next it had followed a course parallel to the northern coast of the continent for which the men were searching with great industry. After a while they were obliged to land on another island for fresh water. They were again entertained by the king of the island. He gave a dinner and a dance in their honor, and they had a chance to admire the graceful motions of the young girls of the villages. They must have been among the Fiji Islands. Farther westward, however, they discovered that the attitude of the natives toward them began to change. Evidently they were reaching a region where the white man was not unknown and was accordingly distrusted.

Chinese and Japanese objects, here and there a knife or a gun of European origin, were found among the natives who came paddling out to the Dutch ship. Their map told them that they were approaching the domains of the East India Company. It had not been their intention to do this, but the reputed Southern continent seemed to be a myth. It was time for them to try and reach home and report their adventures to the owners of the ship.

Sailing along the coast of New Guinea, they at last reached the port of Ternate on the seventeenth of September. Here they found a large Dutch fleet which had just reached the Indies by way of the Strait of Magellan. This fleet was under command of Admiral van Spilbergen, who was much surprised to hear that the Eendracht had reached the Pacific through a new strait. He showed that he did not believe the story which Schouten told of his new discoveries. If there were such a strait, then why had it taken the Eendracht such a long time to reach Ternate? etc. The admiral suspected that this ship was a mere interloper sent by Le Maire to trade in a region where, according to the instructions of the East Indian Company, no other ships than those of the company were allowed to engage in commerce.

This suspicion was very unpleasant for the brave Schouten, but there were other things to worry him. Before the expedition started old Le Maire, a shrewd trader, had thought of the possibility that his ships might not be able to find this unknown continent. In that case he did not want them to come home without some profit to himself, and he had invented a scheme by which he might perhaps beat the company at her own game. The governor-general of the Dutch colonies at that time was a certain Gerard Reynst, who was known to be an avaricious and dishonest official. Le Maire counted upon this, and to his eldest son he had given secret instructions which told him what to do in such circumstances. The idea was very simple. Young Le Maire must bribe Reynst with an offer of money or whatever would be most acceptable to the governor. In return for this Reynst would not be too particular if the Eendracht went to some out-of-the-way island and bought a few hundred thousand pounds worth of spices.

It was a very happy idea, and it undoubtedly would have worked. Unfortunately Reynst had just died. His successor was no one less than Jan Pietersz Coen, the man of iron who was to hammer the few isolated settlements into one strong colonial empire. Coen could not be bribed. To him the law was the law. The Eendracht did not belong to the East India Company; therefore, it had no right to be in India according to Coen's positive instructions. The ship was confiscated. The men were allowed to return to Holland. And the owners were told that they could start a lawsuit in the Dutch courts to decide whether the governor-general had acted within his rights or not.

Young Le Maire sailed for Holland very much dejected. He had lost his father's ship, and nobody would believe him when he told of his great discovery of the new and short connection between the Pacific and the Atlantic. He died on the way home, died of disappointment. His hopes had been so great. He had done his task faithfully, and he and Schouten had found a large number of new islands and had added many thousands of miles of geographical information to that part of the map which was still covered with the ominous letters of terra incognita. Yet through an ordinance which many people did not recognize as just he was deprived of the glory which ought to have come to him. His younger brother reached Holland on the second of July of the year 1617, and a week later he appeared in the meeting of the Estates General. This time the story which he told was believed by his hearers. The idea of an old man being the chief mover in equipping such a wonderful enterprise with the help of his sons and only a small capital against all sorts of odds assured Le Maire the sympathy of the man in the street. For a while Governor-General Coen was highly unpopular.

Old Le Maire started a suit for the recovery of his ship and its contents. After two years of pleading he won his case. The East India Company was ordered to pay back the value of the ship and the goods confiscated. All his official papers were returned to Le Maire. His name and that of the little town of Hoorn, given to the most southern point of the American continent and to the shortest route from the Atlantic to the Pacific, tell of this great voyage of the year 1618.

CHAPTER X
TASMAN EXPLORES AUSTRALIA

It often happened that ships of the Dutch East India Company on their way to the Indies were blown out of their course or were carried by the currents in a southern direction. Then they were driven into a part of the map which was as yet unknown, and they had to find their way about very much as a stranger might do who has left the well-known track of the desert. Sometimes these ships were lost. More often they reached a low, flat coast which seemed to extend both east and west as far as the eye could reach, which offered very little food and very little water, and appeared to be the shore-line of a vast continent which was remarkably poor in both plants and animals. Indeed, so unattractive was this big island, as it was then supposed to be, to the captains of the company that not a single one of them had ever taken the trouble to explore it. They had followed the coast-line until once more they reached the well-known regions of their map, and then they had hastened northward to the comfortable waters of their own Indian Ocean. But of course people talked about this mysterious big island, and they wondered. They wondered whether, perhaps, the stories of the Old Testament, the stories of the golden land of Ophir, which had never yet been found, might not yet be proved true in that large part of the map which showed a blank space and was covered with the letters of terra incognita.

If there were any such land still to be discovered by any European people, the Dutch East India Company decided that they ought to benefit by it. Therefore their directors studied the question with great care and deliberation.

A number of expeditions were sent out one after the other. In the year 1636 two small vessels were ordered to make a careful examination of the island of New Guinea, which was supposed to be the peninsula part of the unknown Southern continent. But New Guinea itself is so large that the two vessels, after spending a very long time along the coast, were obliged to return without any definite information.

Anthony van Diemen, the governor-general of the Dutch East Indies, however, was a man of stubborn purpose, and he refused to discontinue his search until he should have positive knowledge upon this puzzling subject. Six years after this first attempt he appointed a certain Franz Jacobsz Visscher to study the question theoretically from every possible angle and to write him a detailed report. Visscher had crossed the Pacific Ocean a few years after the discovery of Strait Le Maire, and he had visited Japan and China, and was familiar with all the better known parts of the Asiatic seas. He set to work, and he gave the following advice. The ships of the company must take the island of Mauritius as their starting-point. They must follow a southeastern course until they should reach the 54 degree of latitude. If, in the meantime, they had not found any land, they must turn toward the east until they should reach New Guinea, and from there, using this peninsula or island or whatever it was as a starting-point, they should establish its correct relation to the continent of which it was supposed to be a solid part. If it should prove to be an island, then the ships must chart the strait which separated it from the continent, and they must find out whether these did not offer a short route from India to Strait Le Maire and the Atlantic Ocean.

Van Diemen studied those plans carefully. He approved of them, and ordered two ships to be made ready for the voyage. They were small ships. There was the Heemskerk, with sixty men, and the Zeehaen, with only forty. Visscher was engaged to act as pilot and general adviser of the expedition. The command was given to one Abel Tasman. Like most of the great men of the republic, he had made his own career. Born in an insignificant village in the northern part of the republic somewhere in the province of Groningen,—the name of the village was Lutjegat,—he had started life as a sailor, had worked his way up through ability and force of character, and in the early thirties of the seventeenth century he had gone to India. Thereafter he had spent most of his life as captain or mate of different ships of the company. He had been commander of an expedition sent out to discover a new gold-land, which, according to rumor, must be situated somewhere off the coast of Japan, and although he did not find it,—since it did not exist,—he had added many new islands to the map of the company. Since he was a man of very independent character, he was specially fitted to be in command of an expedition which might meet with many unforeseen difficulties.

His instructions gave him absolute freedom of action. The chief purpose of this expedition was a scientific one. Professional draughtsmen were appointed to accompany the Heemskerk and make careful maps of everything that should be discovered. Special attention must be paid to the currents of the ocean and to the prevailing direction of the wind. Furthermore, a careful study of the natives must be made. Their mode of life, their customs, and their habits must be investigated, and they must be treated with kindness. If the natives should come on board and should steal things, the Hollanders must not mind such trifles. The chief aim of the expedition was to establish relations with whatever races were to be discovered. Of course there was little hope of finding anything except long-haired Papuans, but if by any chance Tasman should discover the unknown southland and find that this continent contained the rumored riches, he must not show himself desirous of getting gold and silver. On the contrary, he must show the inhabitants lead and brass, and tell them that these two metals were the most valuable commodities in the country which had sent him upon his voyage. Finally, whatever land was found must be annexed officially for the benefit of the Estates General of the Dutch Republic, and of this fact some lasting memorial must be left upon the coast in the form of a written document, well hidden below a stone or a board planted in such a way that the natives could not destroy it.

On the nineteenth of August, Tasman and his two ships went to Mauritius, where the tanks were filled with fresh water and all the men got a holiday. They were given plenty of food to strengthen them for the voyage which they were about to undertake through the unknown seas. After a month of leisure the two ships left on the sixth of October of the year 1642 and started out to discover whatever they might find. The farther southward they got the colder the climate began to be. Snow and hail and fog were the order of the day. Seals appeared, and everything indicated that they were reaching the Arctic Ocean of the Southern Hemisphere. Day and night they kept a man in the crow's-nest to look for land. Tasman offered a reward of money and rum for the sailor who should first see a light upon the horizon, but they found nothing except salt water and a cloudy sky.

Tasman consulted Visscher, and asked him whether it would not be better to follow the 44 degree of latitude than to go farther into this stormy region. Since they had been sailing in a southern direction for almost a month without finding anything at all, Visscher agreed to this change in his original plans. Once more there followed a couple of weeks of dreary travel without the sight of anything hopeful. At last on the twenty-ninth of November of the year 1642, at four o'clock of the afternoon, land was seen. Tasman thought that it was part of his continent and called it Van Diemen's Land, after the governor-general who had sent him out. We know that it was an island to the south of the Australian continent, and we now call it Tasmania.

On the second of December Tasman tried to go on shore with all his officers, but the weather was bad and the surf was too dangerous for the small boat of the Heemskerk. The ship's carpenter then jumped overboard with the flag of the Dutch Republic and a flagpole under his arm. He reached the shore, planted his pole, and with Tasman and his staff floating on the high waves of the Australian surf and applauding him the carpenter hoisted the orange, white, and blue colors which were to show to all the world that the white man had taken possession of a new part of the world. The carpenter once more swam through the waves, was pulled back into the boat, and the first ceremony connected with the Southern continent was over.

The voyage was then continued, but nowhere could the ships find a safe bay in which they might drop anchor. Everywhere the coast appeared to be dangerous. The surf was high, and the wind blew hard. At last, on the eighteenth of December, after another long voyage across the open sea, more land was seen. This time the coast was even more dangerous than it had been in Tasmania and the land was covered with high mountains. Furthermore the Hollanders had to deal with a new sort of native, much more savage and more able to defend themselves than those who had looked at the two ships from the safe distance of Van Diemen's Land, but had fled whenever the white man tried to come near their shore.

At first the natives of this new land rowed out to the Heemskerk and the Zeehaen and paddled around the ships without doing any harm. But one day the boat of the Zeehaen tried to return their visit. It was at once attacked by the ferocious natives. Three Dutch sailors were killed with clubs, and several were wounded with spears. Not until after the Heemskerk had fired a volley and had sunk a number of canoes did the others flee and leave the Dutch boat alone. The wounded men were taken on board, where several of them died next day. Tasman did not dare to risk a further investigation of this bay with his small vessels, and after the loss of several of his small company he departed. The place of disaster he called Tasman Bay, and sailed farther toward the north. If he had gone a few miles to the east, he would have discovered that this was not a bay at all but the strait which divides the northern and southern part of New Zealand. Now it is called Cook Strait after the famous British sailor who a century later explored that part of the world and who found that New Zealand is not part of a continent, but a large island which offered a splendid chance for a settlement. It was very fertile, and the natives had reached a much higher degree of civilization than those of the Australian continent. Cook made another interesting discovery. The natives who had seen the first appearance of the white man had been so deeply impressed by the arrival of the two Dutch ships that they turned their mysterious appearance into a myth. This myth had grown in size and importance with each new generation, and when Captain Cook dropped anchor off the coast of New Zealand and established relations with the natives, the latter told him a wonderful story of two gigantic vessels which had come to their island ever so long ago, and which had been destroyed by their ancestors while all the men on board had been killed.

It is not easy to follow Tasman on the modern map. After leaving Cook Strait he went northward, and passing between the most northern point of the island, which he called Cape Maria van Diemen, and a small island which, because it was discovered on the sixth of January, was called the "Three Kings Island," he reached open water once more.

He now took his course due north in the hope of reaching some of the islands which Le Maire had discovered. Instead of that, on the nineteenth of January, the two ships found several islands of the Tonga group, also called the Friendly Islands. They baptized these with names of local Dutch celebrities and famous men in the nautical world of Holland. Near one of them, called Amsterdam, because it looked a little more promising than any of the others, the ships stopped, and once more an attempt was made to establish amicable relations with the natives. These came rowing out to the ship, and whenever anything was thrown overboard

they dived after it and showed an ability to swim and to remain under water which ever since has been connected with the idea of the South Sea population. By means of signs and after all sorts of presents, such as little mirrors and nails and small knives, had been thrown overboard to be fished up by the natives, Tasman got into communication with the Tonga people. He showed them a mean, thin chicken and pointed to his stomach. The natives understood this and brought him fresh food. He showed an empty glass and went through the motion of drinking. The natives pointed to the land and showed him by signs that they knew what was wanted, and that there was fresh water to be obtained on shore.

Gradually the natives lost their fear and climbed on board. In exchange for the cocoanuts which they brought they received a plentiful supply of old rusty nails. When those on shore heard that the millennium of useful metal had come sailing into their harbor, their eagerness to get their own share was so great that hundreds of them came swimming out to the Dutch vessels to offer their wares before the supply of nails should be exhausted. Tasman himself went on land, and the relations between native and visitor were so pleasant that the first appearance of the white man became the subject of a Tonga epic which was still recited among the natives when the next European ship landed here a century and a quarter later.

Going from island to island and everywhere meeting with the same sort of long-haired, vigorous-looking men, Tasman now sailed in a south-western direction. He spent several weeks between the Fiji Islands and the group now called Samoa. During all this time his ships were in grave danger of running upon the hidden reefs which are plentiful in this part of the Pacific. At last the winter began to approach and the weather grew more and more unstable, and as the ships after their long voyage were in need of a safe harbor and repair, it was decided to try and return within the confines of the map of the known and explored world. Accordingly the ships sailed westward and discovered several islands of the Solomon group, sailed through the Bismarck Archipelago, as it is called now, and after several months reached the northern part of New Guinea, which they, too, supposed to be the northern coast of the large continent of which they had touched the shores at so many spots, but which instead of the promised Ophir was a dreary, flat land surrounded by little islands full of cocoanuts, natives, and palm-trees, but without a scrap of either gold or silver.

Tasman then found himself in well-known regions. He made straightway for Batavia, and on the fifteenth of June of the year 1644 he landed to report his adventures to the governor-general and the council of the Indian Company. A few months later he was sent out upon a new expedition, this time with three ships. He made a detailed investigation of the northern coast of the real Australian continent. He sailed into the Gulf of Carpentaria. He found the Torres Strait, which he supposed to be a bay between New Guinea and Australia,—for the report of the Torres discovery in 1607 was as yet in the dusty archives of Manila, and had not been given to the world,—and once more he returned by way of the western coast of New Guinea to inform the governor-general that whatever continent he had found produced nothing which could be of any material profit to the Dutch East India Company. In short, New Holland, as Australia was then called, was not settled by the Hollanders because it had no immediate commercial value. After this last voyage no further expeditions were sent out to look for the supposed Southern Continent. From the reports of several ships which had reached the west coast of Australia and from the information brought home by Tasman it was decided that whatever land there might still be hidden between the 110 and 111 degree of longitude, offered no inducements to a respectable trading company which looked for gold and silver and spices, but had no use for kangaroos and the duck-billed platypus. New Holland was left alone until the growing population of the European continent drove other nations to explore this part of the world once more a hundred and twenty years later.

CHAPTER XI
ROGGEVEEN, THE LAST OF THE GREAT VOYAGERS

The Hollanders entered the field of geographical exploration at a late date. The Spaniards and the Portuguese had discovered and navigated distant parts of the world for almost two centuries before the Hollander began to leave his own shores. But when we remember that they were a small nation and were engaged upon one of the most gigantic wars which was ever fought, the result of their labors as pioneers of the map was considerable. They found Spitzbergen and many new islands in the Arctic, and gave us the first reliable information about the impracticability of the North-eastern Passage. They discovered a new route to the Pacific shorter and less dangerous than the Strait of Magellan. They charted the southern part of the Pacific, and made the first scientific inspection of the Australian continent, besides discovering New Zealand and Tasmania. They discovered a number of new islands in the Indian Ocean and settled upon the fertile islands of Mauritius. Of course I now enumerate only the names of their actual discoveries. They established settlements in North and South America and all over Asia and in many places of Africa. They opened a small window into the mysterious Japanese Empire, and got into relation with the Son of Heaven who resided in Peking. They founded a very prosperous colony in South Africa. They had colonies along the Red Sea and the Gulf of Persia. But about these colonies I shall tell in another book. This time I give only the story of the voyages of actual discovery. The adventures of men who set out to perform the work of pioneers, the career of navigators who had convinced themselves that here or there a new continent or an undiscovered cape or a forgotten island awaited their curious eyes, and who then risked their fortunes and their lives to realize their dreams; in one word, the men of constructive vision who are of greater value to their world than any others because they show the human race the road of the future.

In Holland the last of those was a certain Jacob Roggeveen, a man of deep learning, for many years a member of the High Tribunal of the Indies, and a leader among his fellow-beings wherever he went. He had traveled a great deal, and he might have spent the rest of his few years peacefully at home, but when he was sixty-two years old the desire to learn more of the Southern Continent which had been seen, but which had never been thoroughly explored, the wish to know definitely whether there remained anything as yet undiscovered in the Pacific Ocean, drove him across the equator. With three ships and six hundred men he left Texel on the first of August of the year 1721, and the next year in February he was near Juan Fernandez in the Pacific Ocean. An expedition like this had never been seen before. All the experience of past years had been studied most carefully. It was known that people fell ill and died of scurvy because they did not get enough fresh vegetables. Wooden boxes filled with earth were therefore placed along the bulwarks of all the ships. In these some simple and hardy vegetables were planted. Instead of the old method of taking boxes full of bread which turned sour and got moldy, ovens were placed on board, and flour was taken along from which to bake bread. An attempt was made to preserve carrots and beets in boxes filled with powdered peat. People still fell ill during this voyage, but the wholesale death of at least half of the crew of which we read in all the old voyages did not take place. When Roggeveen reached Juan Fernandez he found the cabin of Robinson Crusoe just as it had been left in the year 1709. Otherwise the island proved to be uninhabited. On the seventeenth of March the ships continued their way, and a southern course was taken. Nothing was seen until Easter day, when a new island was found on the spot where an English map hinted at the existence of a large continent. This island, however, contained nothing except a few natives. It did not in the least resemble the unknown Southern Continent of which Roggeveen dreamed. Therefore he went farther toward the south. For a while he followed the route taken many years before by Le Maire. Some of the islands which Le Maire had visited he found on his map. Others he could not locate. Still others were now seen for the first time. It was a very dangerous sea to navigate. The Pacific Ocean is full of reefs. These reefs now appear upon the map, but even in this day of scientific navigation they wreck many a ship. On the nineteenth of April one of Roggeveen's ships ran upon such a hidden reef in the middle of the night. The crew was saved, and was divided among the other two vessels. The ship, however, was a total loss. Nothing could be saved of the personal belongings of the men and the provisions. It is a curious fact that the South Sea islands always have had a wonderful fascination for a certain kind of temperament. Many times while ships crossed the Pacific in the seventeenth and eighteenth century sailors preferred to remain behind on some small island and spend the rest of their lives there with the natives and the fine weather and the long days of lazy ease. Five of Roggeveen's crew remained behind on one of those islands, and when in the year 1764 the British explored the King George Archipelago, they actually found one of these five, then a very old man.

More than half a year was spent by Roggeveen in exploring the hundreds of islands and the many groups of larger islands which the industrious coral insect had built upon the bottom of the ocean. He found the Samoan Islands, and visited several of the Fiji group. Everywhere he met with the same sort of natives. How they got there was a puzzle to Roggeveen. They must have come from some large continent, and he intended to find that continent. But time went by, and his supplies dwindled away, and he did not see anything that resembled his famous continent. Whenever a new peak appeared upon the horizon, there was hope of reaching the land of promise. But from near by the peak always proved to be another rock sticking out of a placid sea, and giving shelter to a few thousand naked savages.

Roggeveen did not stop his search until his men began to get sick and until he had eaten his last piece of bread. Finally, when two-thirds of the crew had died, he considered himself beaten in his search, and after visiting New Guinea he went to the Indies. This expedition, the last one to sail forth to find the land of Ophir of the Old Testament, was a failure. We have been obliged to make the same observation about many of the other voyages which we have described in this little book.

It is true they added some positive knowledge to the map. They located new islands and described rivers and reefs and currents and the velocity or absence of wind in distant parts of the Pacific Ocean; but they always cost the lives of many people, and they ruined the investors in a most cruel fashion.

Yet they had one great advantage: They forced people to leave their comfortable homes. They made them go forth and search for things about which they had had expectant visions. To the rest of the world they gave the tangible sign that in this little Dutch corner of the North Sea there lived a people of enterprise and courage who, although very rich, could yet see beyond mere material gain.

And what more can we ask?

The Author wishes to state his indebtedness to the work of Dr. de Boer, who first of all turned the lengthy and often tedious reports of foreign travel into a concise and readable form and brought the knowledge of these early adventures among a larger number of readers than before. Copies of the voyages in original and reprint can be found in many American libraries. The material for illustrations is very complete. Where no originals were available reprints were made from the pictures which the publishing firm of Meulenhof and Co. of Amsterdam printed in Dr. de Boer's first series of ancient voyages.

THE END